When
FOOTBALL Was
FOOTBALL

Those
WERE The
GAMES

AUTHORS' NOTE:
As far as possible, we have reproduced the reports exactly as they were printed. On occasion this may result in inconsistencies between details in the reports and those in the corresponding "factboxes". Some of the detail may also be absent e.g. attendances.

© Haynes Publishing, 2011

The right of Adam Powley and Richard Havers to be identified as the authors of this Work has been asserted by them in accordance with the Copyright, Designs & Patents Act 1988.

All rights reserved. No part of this publication may be reproduced, stored in a retrieval system or transmitted, in any form or by any means, electronic, mechanical, photocopying, recording or otherwise, without prior permission in writing from the publisher.

First published in 2011

A catalogue record for this book is available from the British Library

ISBN: 978-0-857331-68-7

Published by Haynes Publishing, Sparkford, Yeovil,
Somerset BA22 7JJ, UK
Tel: 01963 442030 Fax: 01963 440001
Int. tel: +44 1963 442030 Int. fax: +44 1963 440001
E-mail: sales@haynes.co.uk
Website: www.haynes.co.uk

Haynes North America Inc., 861 Lawrence Drive,
Newbury Park, California 91320, USA

Images © Mirrorpix

Creative Director: Kevin Gardner
Designed for Haynes by BrainWave

Printed and bound in the US

When
FOOTBALL *Was*
FOOTBALL

Those
WERE *The*
GAMES

A Nostalgic Look at a Century of Great Football Matches

Adam Powley and Richard Havers

INTRODUCTION

Like most boys growing up in the 1970s, I dreamed of becoming a professional footballer. A lack of talent meant that fantasy would never come true, though the bewildering careers of some overrated modern players give me hope. Still, if I couldn't play the game, maybe the next best thing was to write about it?

Back then, my heroes weren't just Glenn Hoddle, Steve Perryman, Johan Cruyff and Roberto Rivelino. It was the men who told me about how these god-like superstars played. In particular the great football scribes who wrote for our family newspaper, the *Daily Mirror*. While most kids had pictures of the footballing greats of the day on their walls, I was cutting out the match reports of Frank McGhee, Harry Miller, Ken Montgomery and their colleagues.

This book is in no small part a celebration of men like McGhee and their predecessors at the *Mirror*; men armed only with shorthand notes, clattering typewriters and their genius. Not forgetting, of course, the photographers. Because these men (female football writers and snappers were virtually unheard of, save for the magnificent Julie Welch) made football games come alive.

In an era when the FA Cup final and some internationals were the only live matches on TV, newspaper match reports were truly essential reading. There was no 24-hour rolling sports news, no dedicated radio stations and no internet to fill the gap. If you were not there in person to see the actual game, reading the wonderful descriptions of the action and the shrewd analysis of the play made you feel as if you *were* there.

Over the course of the following collection of match reports and photos, we pay tribute to the crack football team at the *Mirror* and its sister paper the *Sunday Mirror*. Starting at the turn of the 20th century and continuing almost up to the present day, we showcase the great matches, the pivotal games, the famous victories and the lesser-known contests that tell the vivid story of a century of football.

Together they reveal a different football world and how that world evolved. It's possible to trace the development in tactics through these reports, from the twin full-backs of the 1900s to the Dutch brand of Total Football. It's fascinating also to see how the whole football business has changed, from brief mentions of contracts and transfer fees to the saturation coverage of every aspect of the sport that we see today (though, interestingly, gate receipts have always been highlighted).

The style of football reporting has also evolved. In the early days wingers were "enterprising and virile", while players in any position were always called just by their surname. Crowds would occasionally go "mad with excitement" and errors were treated with a brutal and very succinct honesty: if a corner kick was wasted, well, the reporter would simply write "it was useless."

Early reports tended to have much longer paragraphs and provided minute detail about incidents and passages of play – note that more modern reports carry a good deal more opinion from the writer, a reflection of the fact that readers can now see for themselves what has actually happened.

Technology has also changed. The old days of hard copy, shorthand, copy takers, and runners have given way to instant reports posted online with second by second updates, full coverage of press conferences and teams of reporters at one game – with the facilities to match.

I was one of that luckier journalistic generation to have such tools at my disposal. Having spent some time as a match reporter with the *Sunday Mirror* I achieved at least part of my childhood football dream. In doing so my respect for those writers who had gone before me was strengthened. Condensing the thrill and drama of 90 minutes of football action is not quite as straightforward as it might seem, but masters like McGhee, Miller and co. made it look easy.

Adam Powley

Growing up in those far-off days before even *Match of the Day*, (and once it did arrive on our television screens football was strictly rationed), it was the thrill of reading newspaper reports while doing my paper-round that filled me with information, facts and figures about the game. Like many people I took it all for granted that the words just somehow made it onto the page, purely to inform and entertain me. I still love reading a great match report, even when I've watched the game on the telly. Somehow great football writers have a knack of encapsulating a game in such an appealing way.

When I had the idea for *Those Were The Games* it was simply to find great writing about great games. In the pages of the *Daily Mirror* it hasn't been hard to do.

Richard Havers

Everton keeper Andy Rankin makes a save from Leeds striker Jimmy Greenhoff watched by Peter Storrie in April 1966.

Football Reporting Old Style

FOOTBALL RESULTS

After going through the first two months of the season without experiencing defeat in the First and Second Leagues, Sheffield United and Woolwich Arsenal, the respective leaders, both sustained there first reverse on Saturday at the feet of Aston Villa and Barnsley. The two Sheffield teams are still at the head of the Premier Association competition, but Preston North End, having won their match against Grimsby, are now the legitimate leaders of the Second Division.

Corinthians played a tie with Millwall of three goals each; the Casuals beat the Dark Blues by three goals to one; but the Light Blues defeated Middlesex by three to nil.

Queen's Park Rangers and Fulham played a draw of one goal each in the Association Cup; and in the same competition West Ham beat Brighton and Hove by four goals to nil.

1905 14th February

Wolverhampton 1 Sunderland 0

Some sensation was caused in football circles in Sunderland yesterday by the news that Common, the international inside-right, had been transferred from the Sunderland club to Middlesbrough, as was reported, and inquiries went to confirm the belief, that the sum paid by Middlesbrough for Common's transfer was £1,000.

COMMON'S LAST GAME FOR S'LAND

Having played a draw of one goal each on Sunderland's ground on Saturday, the latter team met Wolverhampton Wanderers yesterday at the Molineux Grounds, Wolverhampton.

There were fully 18,000 people present. During the opening half the exchanges were very fast, and the Wanderers played a brilliant game. Taking a corner kick, Hopkins on one occasion shot into the net, but the ball did not touch a second player, and consequently the goal was not allowed.

Later on Smith failed by inches to score for the home side. Sunderland frequently broke away, and Common did some splendid work, but the Wanderers' defence was too sound. At the interval nothing had been scored.

Play in the second half was decidedly in favour of Sunderland at first. Common, who was in superb form, being frequently dangerous.

The home forwards then got away and made a desperate attack on the Sunderland goal. The effort was attended with success, Smith beating Webb with a magnificent shot, amid an indescribable scene of excitement. A little later Smith missed an open goal, and, as it turned out, nothing more was scored. Wolverhampton Wanderers, who had five men temporarily injured, thus won by one goal to nil.

FA Cup First Round Replay	
Wolverhampton... 1 Smith	Sunderland... 0
	Att: 18,000

Alf Common.

1912 5th May

Charity Game for a Disaster

TITANIC FUND FOOTBALL

ROVERS WIN ENGLISH CHARITY SHIELD BY BEATING RANGERS AT TOTTENHAM

Blackburn Rovers 2 QPR 1

In the extra week sanctioned by the Football Association in order that matches could be played for the benefit of the fund that is being raised for the sufferers of the Titanic disaster, the ruling body ordered their Charity Shield match, between Blackburn Rovers, the champions of the Football League, and Queen's Park Rangers, the champions of the Southern League, to be decided on the ground of the Tottenham Hotspur Club.

The proceeds will go to the fund, but, unfortunately, the contribution will not be so big as had been anticipated. A miserable drizzle fell in London all day, and the bankings behind the goals were very thin with spectators.

The rain softened the ground for the players, and an interesting game was seen, Blackburn Rovers deservedly beating the Southern Leaguers by two goals to one.

The Rovers were the more forceful side all through, but it has to be added that the combination of the Rangers' forwards, especially during the first half, was distinctly good. The Rovers, who had Aitkenhead at centre-forward, pressed at the start,

The Titanic prior to her maiden voyage.

but, the men who shot for goal had no luck.

Early on Revill, the Rangers' inside-right, had an excellent chance, with only Robinson to beat, but he sent the ball straight at the goalkeeper. Directly after, and about a quarter of an hour following the start, Revill gave the Rangers the lead. The ball rose from his foot to the top of the net, and Robinson had little chance of getting at it.

Revill sent the ball into the net a second time, but on the advice of one of the linesmen the referee disallowed the goal for offside. One minute from the change of ends Aitkenhead equalised for the Rovers.

The First Leaguers played strongly during the second half, and after Bradshaw, their half-back, had struck the crossbar with a long shot, Clennell rushed the winning goal for them. This happened about twenty minutes from the finish.

The official return gave the gate as 7,000, the receipts being £260. A collection realised £4.

FA Charity Shield

Blackburn Rovers... ( ) 2	QPR... (0) 1
Aitkenhead 44	Revill 15
Clennell 70	

Att: 7,000

EA Cup Marathon

BRILLIANT CUP VICTORY FOR SUNDERLAND

NEWCASTLE UNITED BEATEN BY THREE GOALS TO NOTHING IN A BLIZZARD AT ST. JAMES'S PARK – TWO GOALS FOR MORDUE

Newcastle 0 Sunderland 3

P.J. Moss

After five hours of Cup fighting Sunderland qualified to meet Burnley at Blackburn in the semi-final-round of the English Cup. It was really a wonderful game, and Sunderland should have won by more than three goals to nil.

No such an ending could have been expected after the first match at Sunderland, when the Newcastle half-backs dominated the play. But from match to match Sunderland improved, until today the forwards shook off the attentions of Veitch, Low and Hay and both when playing with the blizzard at their back and when facing it they were always too clever for the Newcastle defence. Indeed, Sunderland had many more scoring chances in the second half than they did in the first.

That interest in the strenuous struggle was evidenced by the fact that as early as nine o'clock crowds of excursionists from Wearside, sporting the Sunderland colours, were parading the streets of the city. It was bitterly cold, and snow showers and sunshine alternated an hour before the start of a veritable blizzard swept over the district, but by this time there were over 40,000 people on the ground, and, in spite of the rigours of the weather, a steady stream was pouring towards St. James's Park from all quarters of the city.

Sunderland had exactly the same side as played in the two previous games, but Newcastle had to rearrange their team. The backs and half-backs were the same as in the previous matches, but Duncan and Stewart came into the forward line in place of McDonald and Shepherd. Stewart had played in the first match at Sunderland, so with the exception that Rutherford was absent Newcastle thus played their full strength, which does not lend much colour to the story that they played a reserve side against Blackburn Rovers on Saturday on account of injuries to their players.

Mr. Baker again had charge of the game and refereed badly, tempers being lost on both sides because the players were not allowed to contest the game in a sporting spirit. But Sunderland rose superior to it all, and I have never seen finer football played under such deplorable conditions.

Holley, at inside-left, who would have been playing at Bristol but for this Cup-tie, was the best of a fast, enterprising and virile line of forwards, but now and again the combination of Cuggy, Mordue and Buchan, on the other wing, was cheered to the echo.

Mordue's goal in the second half was the result of this wonderful work, and the Newcastle defenders were left standing still, nonplussed and helpless when the final touch

Bathers ready to take a dip in the North Sea at Roker Sunderland on Christmas morning 1913. We wonder how many of them went to the games?

was put on. Richardson was a bustling centre, and Martin was a great winger, doing some fine individual work against McCracken.

Thomson again led his men with rare judgment, and played another stirring game. I should say he is certain of his Scottish cap again. Cuggy and Low were less conspicuous, but sound, and Gladwin and Milton this time made no mistakes. Butler, in goal, had only a couple of anxious times and on both occasions he got the ball away well.

Lawrence made many good saves in the Newcastle goal, and McCracken and Hudspeth both defended splendidly, but McCracken limped a bit in the second half, and was frequently beaten for pace.

The Newcastle halves had an off day. Perhaps they played as well as they were allowed to do, but they were outpaced all the time. The forwards were clever at times but did better against the wind than with it. Hibbert and Duncan were the pick, McTavish got in some nice work now and again, but there were only a few bouts of brilliant passing such as we expect from Newcastle.

It is still a far cry to the final, but if we get Sunderland and the Villa there, what a game it will be, probably the best on record at the Palace. But you never can tell.

Sunderland won the toss and had the wind in the first half.

Newcastle's goal was in danger early on when McCracken fouled Martin, and three corners fell to Sunderland in the course of the next minute. Play was scrambling at the start, and it was not improved by Mr. Baker at once absolutely putting the veto on fair shoulder charges.

Eight minutes after the start Sunderland scored. The ball was cleverly worked in by Richardson who passed to Holley. The latter's shot was a soft one, and Low, in trying to kick clear, sent the ball hard against Holley, whence it rebounded through the goal. Just after McCracken brought Buchan down, and both were hurt.

Now and again Newcastle got down against the wind and danger threatened the Sunderland goal from a well placed corner kick, which Thomson headed away. The Sunderland forwards were now playing fine football, and Martin shot across the Newcastle goal with a good low shot.

Another blizzard swept the ground, and Sunderland, with it behind them, redoubled their efforts. It was now one continuous solo on the whistle and the players on both sides were roughing it, Wilson and Gladwin having to be forcibly pulled apart by their colleagues.

Wilson, who had kicked Gladwin got the worst of the encounter and apparently had his ribs hurt in a bear's hug; and so Wilson and also McCracken were both on the injured list before the game was half an hour old.

In a desperate dash on the Sunderland goal Thomson only just cleared. Then Holley got through for Sunderland, but the referee adjudged that he had knocked the ball through and the point was disallowed.

Against the blizzard the Newcastle defence were superb but they were hard pushed and did anything to get the ball away. Martin was tripped by Veitch four minutes from the interval, and Mordue scored from the penalty kick giving Sunderland a two goals lead at half-time.

"Now then, boys, stand on no ceremony; get it away anyhow. There's only three quarters of an hour to go." So said Charlie Thomson as he led his men out of the dressing room after the breather.

The snow had ceased, and Sunderland started well, Buchan

Newcastle United, Cup winners, greeted outside Central Station in Newcastle on 29th April 1910 when they brought home the Cup. Thousands massed on the streets of Tyneside to welcome the team home.

hitting the post from a corner kick. The ball was kept in front of the Newcastle goal, and Buchan miskicked with a goal at his mercy.

Butler once saved the Sunderland goal by throwing the ball behind when three forwards were on top of him, and a couple of corners followed before Cuggy cleared. Newcastle were now making desperate efforts, but the Sunderland backs played with confidence born of a lead of two goals.

Mordue got through once and passed to Richardson right in front of goal but although it was a backward pass, Richardson was given offside. Lawrence had to save from Holley, and

FA Cup Fourth Round Quarter-final Second Replay

Newcastle... 0   Sunderland... 3

Holley 8
Mordue 41 (pen), 80

Att: 40,000

Butler got the ball away from a close range shot by Hibbert – a lucky escape for Sunderland.

More corners fell to Newcastle, but, desperate as was the onslaught of the Newcastle men, the Sunderland defence was just as desperate. After a brilliant run and centre by Martin, both Richardson and Mordue had the easiest of chances of scoring a third goal for Sunderland, but Richardson's shot was a soft one and Lawrence saved at full length.

The goalkeeper, however, got a nasty kick in the head from Richardson, who followed up his shot and fell over Lawrence as he lay on the ground, after some bewildering passing between Mordue, Buchan and Cuggy. Mordue scored a brilliant goal for Sunderland, and settled the issue.

Sunderland had four backs and Newcastle eight forwards in the last few minutes, but it was all over now, and the best team in England had won after one of the most interesting and exciting series of matches in the whole history of the English Cup. It was champion football played by a champion team, which did not, from goalkeeper to outside-left, have a single weak spot.

The gate receipts amounted to £3,030, and Newcastle must find some consolation in the fact that they have shared £11,000 in this season's competition.

Games on Battlefield

THIS MORNING'S GOSSIP

HOW THE FOOTBALL FUND GOES

"The Rambler"

Thirteen more footballs arrived yesterday, so we are able to close the year with the fine total of 765, which is sixty-five better than I had hoped for. We are getting them off to the soldiers as hard as we can, but the applications still pour in, and we shall want the thousand balls if we are to satisfy all those who ask. Up to date we have been able to satisfy every applicant from the front.

Among my football letters yesterday was one from the Coldstream Guards at the front. No. 3 Company evidently numbers in its muster a poet, who writes that he and his comrades have played the Prussian Guard their return game at Ypres and beat them easily. The first game took place on the Aisne. Then he continues :-

We kicked off sharply at daybreak with a good old English cheer,
We advanced on their goal – passed the half-backs and the goalkeeper tried hard to clear;
He saved his side, true, from destruction; our forwards shot splendid and true,
And surely their side got disheartened and gave up all hope and – Adieu.
We passed all the great opposition, we knew we could score if we did,
So we played the game of our life, sir, for Justice we made our bid.
We shot at the goal and succeeded, we scored though the "goalie" was tall,
So perhaps you'll consider this letter and send us just one prized football.

He gets one; it went off yesterday.

Two regimental football teams playing a match at the front. General Briggs will give a prize of £5 to the winner of the British Trenches League.

British soldiers seen here leaving their trench to meet their German opponents on Christmas Day 1914 to play a game of football. The truce began on Christmas Eve when German troops began decorating the area around their trenches in the region of Ypres, Belgium for Christmas.

WHY THEY LOST

Another of day letters gave a racy account of a match played on Christmas Day within sight of the firing line, between the Lincolns and a team of ambulance men. Says the writer, one of the Lincolns: "Owing to the large amount of Christmas pudding sent us from home, we were beaten by six to two."

Then he adds a postscript: "P.S. – The referee being a stretcher bearer accounts for the high score against us."

ANY OFFERS?

And then another cheerful "Tommy" writes that as soon as the ball arrived he and his comrades had a match with a neighbouring corps and beat them five to nil. "A good beginning," he says, "and we are now challenging any club in England. So, if you hear of any team wishing a match, send 'em out here with rifles and we will show them how to play two games."

WE WANT 1,000 NOW

So you see, "Tommy" still wants footballs and when he gets them, he appreciates them. We must get a thousand for him.

POSTSCRIPT

The feature in "This Morning's Gossip" showed how, even in the terrible midst of the First World War, football was still a central part of men's lives. While the sport had come in for criticism at the start of the conflict for the continuation of league fixtures (suspended in 1915), some among the top brass realised the morale-boosting potential of the game and sanctioned matches among the troops.

Impromptu games also took place between enemy troops during temporary ceasefires; the 17th Battalion of the Middlesex regiment was made up of footballers; and some soldiers from the London Irish Rifles even dribbled a football as they went "over the top" during an attack on enemy lines.

Soldiers of the Army Service Corps in France seen here playing football in their time away from the front. Circa 1915.

The Magic of the Cup

BOLTON'S GREAT CUP VICTORY

HUGE CROWD SEES WEST HAM UNITED BEATEN IN WEMBLEY'S FIRST FINAL BY 2-0

Bolton 2 West Ham 0

Bolton Wanderers emerged successful from the most amazing Cup final ever played when they defeated West Ham United in the new Empire Stadium ground yesterday by two clear goals, and won the trophy for the first time in their history. They were the better side throughout and fully deserved their victory.

Despite the arrangements that had been made to accommodate a record crowd, the spectators were almost out of hand an hour before the start. Hundreds rushed on to the track and up to the goal-line while many invaded the field itself.

Half an hour before the time fixed for starting there were fully 10,000 people on the playing pitch, and at this point it was feared that the match would not be started until long after the arranged time, if at all.

It was only after very great difficulty that the pitch was cleared, and the players themselves added their efforts to those of the police and Mr. Wall, the secretary of the Football Association, in inducing the crowd to get off the playing area. The players were presented to the King and it was forty-four minutes after

ALL READY FOR TO-DAY'S EAGERLY ANTICIPATED

Smith.

Rowley.

Finney.

Seddon.

Joe Smith, accomplished inside forward, who captains the Bolton Wanderers.

Bolton Wanderers practise the winning shot on a billiard table.

Bolton Wanderers with the mascot "cat" which they brought from

How the Stadium looks from the air, showing extent of the covered stands.

Pym.　Jack.　Jennings.　Vizard.　J. R. Smith.

It is very possible that all Cup final attendance records will be broken to-day when West Ham and the Bolton Wanderers meet at the magnificent new Wembley Stadium. On no previous occasion has general interest been more keen, and testing teams will largely swell the crowds that wi

the arranged time when Watson kicked off for West Ham.

The first movement was by Bolton, J. R. Smith taking a long pass from Jennings on the run, which was kicked down into touch. Vizard tried a long shot from the throw-in, but it went into the crowd.

Page 9

FOR THE FOOTBALL ASSOCIATION'S CUP AT THE NEW WEMBLEY STADIUM

of West Ham, in a characteristic display of energy. It will be understood that the men have to be trained to a fine point of fitness to endure this sort of thing.

Hufton, the West Ham goalkeeper, clearing a hot shot while training.

Mrs. Tresadern, wife of the West Ham player, on their little farm at Epping. The team has adopted her for its mascot.

George Kay, West Ham's centre half and captain, is a tower of strength.

Kay.

Henderson.

Bishop.

Ruffell.

Assnt. of West Brom. who will referee the con— at Wembley to-day.

The Cup which is to be fought for by the representatives of North and South.

A general view of the Stadium taken from the top of one of the stands.

Butler.

Brown.

Watson.

Moore.

Tresadern.

Richards.

Young.

Hufton.

n provides one of the con— field of combat.

Stadium has accommodation for upwards of 125,000 spectators and there is every indication that its resources will be taxed to the utmost. Barring last-minute accidents, both teams will take

the field in full strength and there is the prospect of a mighty struggle before the issue is decided, and the coveted Cup is won.

JACK'S EARLY GOAL

Then came the turn of the West Ham right-wing, where Richards and Brown made a run, which Finney terminated. Bolton got going at once, and Seddon sent a long pass up for Jack to run through and score a somewhat easy goal, in three minutes.

Hufton had little chance and his backs were badly placed.

At once West Ham retaliated, Watson and Moore playing nicely. The centre forced a corner, from which he might have scored but he ballooned the ball over the bar from five yards range.

Neat combined work by the West Ham left-wing gave Howarth some trouble, and when Bolton got down again Jack was offside. Tresadern was conspicuous for forcible, work that sent West Ham in again, but Ruffell was plainly afraid to trust himself with the crowd actually on the line and in some places over it.

At the north side they were many yards inside the field, and the play had to be suspended in order to get the crowd back.

DANGEROUS HAMMERS

It was twelve minutes before play could be recommenced, and thus far only eleven minutes actual play had taken place. West Ham got away on the right, where Bishop sent

Richards off to force a corner, which was useless. At the time Richards fell full speed into the crowd. Offside against Vizard held up a Bolton run at a critical moment, but J. Smith, with a pass, sent Vizard off again although all he could do was to run the ball into the crowd.

19

A beautiful movement by Richards on the right almost saw a West Ham goal, for Bishop, after speedy and pretty work, shot hard, and Pym, after fumbling and falling, managed to get the ball away with Watson and Brown converging on him while he was on his knees. Away went Bolton to the other end. J. H. Smith and Jack playing nice football, but Henderson, who was playing superbly, stopped them.

A long centre from Vizard saw the ball crossed to Butler. The right-winger returned it and Smith kicked it into the net, but just at this point was given offside. Vizard lobbed a free kick nicely into the front of the goal, where Kay and Young had much difficulty to get it away from the persistent Jack. The two Smiths carried Bolton up again, and only very fine work by Tresadern kept the Bolton captain out. A corner forced off Henderson was next cleared.

Watson then got away for West Ham, but could not control a lively ball, and Finney cleared with great coolness. Ruffell had to yield up a lovely pass from Watson to Howarth, who got speedily to the ball, and a minute later Butler rushed away from Seddon's pass, only to lose the ball, which bounded awkwardly to Tresadern. Moore twice passed nicely to Ruffell, who found Howard a very stubborn back, and when Bolton worked along again Vizard miskicked in the penalty area in front of goal.

Neat work by Watson was wasted when he passed to Richards, who was too well attended by Finney to do anything with the ball. Offside against Moore spoiled a subsequent effort, but kicking by the West Ham backs kept their men on the offensive and again a forward pass spoiled West Ham's chances. This was the last incident before half-time, when Bolton still led by a goal to nil.

The teams merely changed round and went straight on, Watson threatening to go through on his own in the first minute.

CHAOS AT CUP-TIE FINAL: WHO WAS TO BLAME?

The Daily Mirror

NET SALE MUCH THE LARGEST OF ANY DAILY PICTURE NEWSPAPER

24 PAGES

No. 6,079. Registered at the G.P.O. as a Newspaper. MONDAY, APRIL 30, 1923. One Penny.

POLICE v. CROWD: WEMBLEY'S FIRST CUP FINAL

A remarkable photograph, taken from the air, of the Stadium at Wembley, with spectators swarming over the playing pitch, while hundreds are clustered outside.

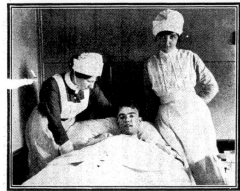

Arnold Ratcliffe, of Bolton. He was crushed and picked up unconscious.

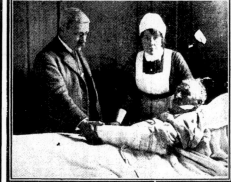

Thomas McGrigor, of Islington, in hospital with a broken arm and leg.

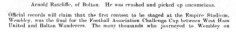

Official records will claim that the first contest to be staged at the Empire Stadium, Wembley, was the final for the Football Association Challenge Cup between West Ham United and Bolton Wanderers. The many thousands who journeyed to Wembley on

Saturday will, however, long retain the memory of an earlier struggle in which the opposing elements were police and public, the ultimate victory resting with the force, whose untiring efforts eventually produced order from utter chaos.

ESCAPES FOR BOLTON

Some clever football by Richards, Brown and Watson served West Ham well, although nothing came of it, and the Bolton left-wing next flushed into prominence, which similarly fizzled out when within striking distance, through Smith failing to control the ball.

A bad foul by Jennings on Richards almost brought about the downfall of the Bolton goal, for first Watson shot into Pym's hands and then Moore, while falling, shot straight at the Bolton goalie. A run down by Vizard did not promise much, but he passed, and J. R. Smith, dashing up, shot into the top of the net, the ball bouncing out of the goal again. It was a beautiful goal for Bolton, and came seven minutes in the second half.

After this Bolton appeared to slow up but it cannot be said that West Ham put on speed, although they certainly played with more precision, a quality that had not been very prominent hitherto. Too often their passing was wild and straight to a Bolton defender. Twice Watson got offside when better things for West Ham were promised.

Good work by Bishop stopped a run by Vizard and a poor pass by Watson, in front of goal gave Pym much relief.

PLAY DETERIORATES

Jennings handled in his own half, but once more West Ham's kick was spoiled by Finney, whose ability to trap the ball was remarkable. Jack and Butler got down on the right, but the winger, after losing the ball, fouled Young and the Londoners' goal gained relief. The pace of the football as well as its quality had deteriorated a lot and some reeling crept into the game.

A bad foul by Jennings near the goal gave West Ham a free kick, and Henderson, who took the kick sent it skimming at a great pace inches over the bar. Free kicks were rather too frequent at this period, and the Londoners gained valuable ground at times, to lose it, as a rule, by hasty passing. A nice kick by Watson sent Ruffell in, but Finney came across to effect a glorious save.

West Ham were now making a real effort to stave off the imminent defeat, but so fine were the Bolton backs that Pym was rarely troubled. Some scuffling play in midfield saw Richards break away, but a reckless kick sent the ball over the line.

J. R. Smith nearly got through at the other end, where Henderson brought him down with a very heavy charge and it was some time before he could resume. Down came Bolton again, and Jack had a great shot beautifully saved by Hufton, although the Bolton forward was given offside in the meantime.

THE KING PRESENTS CUP

Bolton made little use of a free kick from a long throw, and Watson forced a corner off Finney, Seddon heading it away very truly, and Joe Smith sent the speedy Vizard off. A series of throw-ins brought the game to a conclusion, Bolton being deservedly the winners by two goals to nil.

At the conclusion of the game, which, despite the trouble, stands officially as the Cup final, the King presented the cup to J. Smith, the Bolton captain and the medals to the players. There was an enormous crowd in front of the royal box, and the King was the object of an ovation that can rarely have been heard on a football ground. The fervour with which the National Anthem was sung was in the highest degree inspiring. In an official statement issued by the exhibition authorities, it was estimated that over 150,000 were present inside the stadium.

POSTSCRIPT

The first FA Cup final staged at Wembley was also one of the most dramatic – if not for the game then for the vast crowds that packed into the ground to try to get a glimpse of the play. Henceforth Cup Finals became all-ticket affairs.

Given the size of the crowd, it is almost a miracle that there were no fatalities, and indeed most of the two dozen or so people who were hospitalised suffered relatively minor injuries. That in large part was due to the good nature of the spectators and Billie, the white horse ridden by PC Scorey, who together did much to restore order.

FA Cup Final

Bolton Wanderers... (1) 2   West Ham Utd... (0) 0
Jack 3
J.R. Smith 52

Att: 126,047 (official; est. 150,000-200,000)

Footballing Veteran

VETERAN FOOTBALLERS STILL SCORING CUP GOALS

MEREDITH AND FLEMING IN WINNING TEAMS

Brighton 1 Manchester City 6

Two veterans of football helped to bring about the only real surprises in Saturday's Cup-ties.

Meredith, on the verge of fifty, assisted Manchester City in their great 6-1 victory at Brighton, and Fleming scored the winning goal for Swindon against the Palace at Selhurst. London lost its sole surviving club in the latter game, and Cardiff are now the only real menace to the Northern clubs.

POSTSCRIPT

In his second spell with City, the great Billy Meredith was still banging them in at the age of forty-nine. One of the biggest stars of the early 20th century for City and their rivals Manchester United, Meredith had co-founded the Players Union (forerunner of the PFA) and was an iconic figure in the development of the game.

1927 23rd April

The Welsh Conquer England

HOW ENGLAND'S FOOTBALL CUP WENT TO WALES

LEWIS'S FATAL SLIP BRINGS ARSENAL'S DISASTER

Arsenal 0 Cardiff City 1

P.J. Moss

Cardiff City beat the Arsenal by a goal to nothing at Wembley on Saturday before the King and 91,000 of his lieges, and so took the English Cup out of the country for the first time in its eventful history.

It was a poor game, and a fluke goal decided the issue. The great feature of the contest was the superb and heroic defence of the Cardiff backs and half-backs. And of these Hardy stood out head and shoulders above his fellows.

The Arsenal had the balance of play in the first half, when they attacked almost incessantly. But there was little constructive play, and the Cardiff half-backs kept up a smashing game which swept aside all efforts at combination.

Buchan and Hulme were more than held by little Hardy. He always seemed to get his kick in the nick of time, and his skilful positioning was almost uncanny in its accuracy.

Where the ball went on the Cardiff left-wing there was Hardy, either in attack or defence, and the huge crowd cheered him as one man. Even the Arsenal's partisans had to give England's best half-back a share of their applause.

FA councillors on the Selection Committee who have always refused to crown the little man's sterling play with an international cap must have wondered what they have been doing since the war in passing him over.

On the right-wing Keenor was dour, determined and fast.

Brain, in the Arsenal centre, had a very lean time. He did not get those nice push-through passes from Buchan or Blyth, and Hulme and Hoar rarely got in centres which were any good to him. When the ball did reach him it was generally in the air and difficult to control.

CORNERS FOR ARSENAL

Sloan, the Cardiff centre-half, too, shadowed him all the while,

so that although the Arsenal attacked for the most part, they rarely looked like scoring. At one time in the first half they took five corners in five minutes, but the ball never went kindly for them.

Next to Hardy, I thought Parker, the Arsenal right-back, was the most outstanding figure on the field. He scarcely made a mistake in a hard game, and with the Arsenal half-backs not so good as the Cardiff trio he had more to do.

Cardiff player Billy Hardy forces his way through the crowd.

unhampered by opposing players. He rose to his knees, apparently intending to throw the ball away; slipped; it fell out of his hands and trickled towards goal.

Lewis scrambled after the ball, but could not reach it before it crossed the fatal white line, and by that fluky goal Cardiff took the Cup to Wales.

At least twice Farquharson in the Cardiff goal dropped the ball, but without disaster to his side. And once in punching out from a free kick by Parker he only half hit the ball and it slithered off his hand for a corner kick.

Kennedy, who filled Cope's place at left-back, came through the ordeal with flying colours. He played like a veteran, and was always cool if not so resourceful as Parker.

The Cardiff backs were uneven. Watson at times seemed scared, and kicked anywhere and anyhow so long as he got rid of the ball; but Nelson was splendid.

Cardiff's forwards were very moderate. They did little in the way of combined play, and, like the Arsenal, it is "first time" with them always.

So the match was singularly devoid of incident and the actual goal scored by Cardiff was in itself a tragedy for Lewis.

Twenty-nine minutes of the second half had slipped by, and we were talking of extra time being played, when Cardiff in one of their attacks got away on the left. Len Davies pushed the ball into the centre to Ferguson, and he drove it in from about the penalty line.

Another incident was when Sloan took a big kick towards the Cardiff left-wing. From a distance of a couple of yards the ball took Butler on the point, and he was as cleanly knocked out as if a boxer had chinned him for the count!

After the goal the Arsenal strove desperately for an equaliser, and once Buchan and Brain nearly did the trick, but the nearest to a second goal in the match came when Curtis, the Cardiff outside-right, got clean through the defence, and then kicked yards wide of the target.

So ended a very poor final tie. Nerves told their tale on both sides and play was always below First League standard.

THE WINNING SHOT

In making a good save Lewis fell full-length, and onto the ball. He was quite a couple of yards outside his goal and

FA Cup Final	
Arsenal... (0) 0	Cardiff City... ( ) 1
	Lewis (o.g.) 74
	Att: 91,000

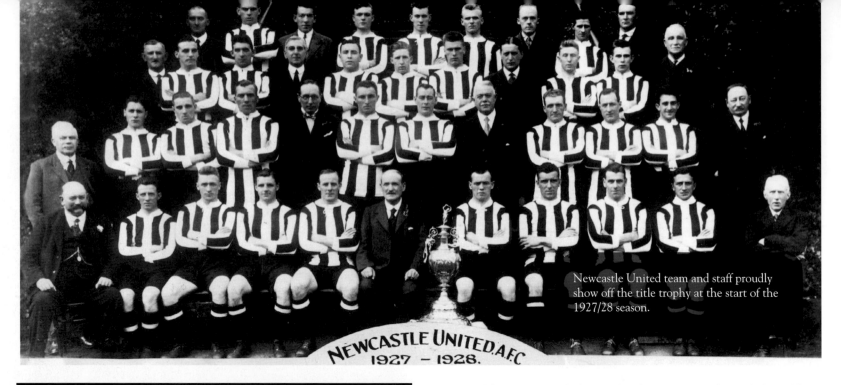

Newcastle United team and staff proudly show off the title trophy at the start of the 1927/28 season.

A Remarkable Fixture at St. James's Park

BLIZZARD AND 12 GOALS ON TYNESIDE

Newcastle 7 Aston Villa 5

Football's greatest foe on Saturday was winter's icy blasts. Two games were temporarily held up through snowstorms and attendances dropped to 530,000. First Leaguers seemed to exult in the conditions. Newcastle and the Villa ran riot at St. James's Park, crowding on twelve goals.

Tyneside was mantled in snow, but Newcastle and the Villa warmed up the 25,000 spectators.

Newcastle opened in tornado fashion, sweeping the Villa off their feet and registering three goals through Seymour, McDonald and McCurley within one minute.

When the Villa regained their breath Cook got one home for them. Wilkinson, who deputises for Gallacher, scored the Geordies' fourth, and Waring, a Tranmere product, made the Villa's crop two before the interval.

In the whirling snow, which fell faster in the second half, McCurley hooked in a fifth goal, and Wilkinson two more for Newcastle.

The Villa wound up this sensational scoring match, the heaviest in the First Division this season, with three goals in twelve minutes through Waring, Dorrell and York.

Olney was injured towards the close and Gibson went into the Villa's goal.

Football League Division One

Newcastle... (4) 7	Aston Villa... (2) 5
Seymour	Cook
McDonald	Waring 2
McCurley 2	Dorrell
Wilkinson 3	York

1928 Saturday 5th May

Tightest Points Spread in English Football & Record Goals in a Season by a Player

SHEFFIELD JOY BELLS TOLL A KNELL FOR SPURS

DRAMATIC CLIMAX TO GREAT FOOTBALL SEASON

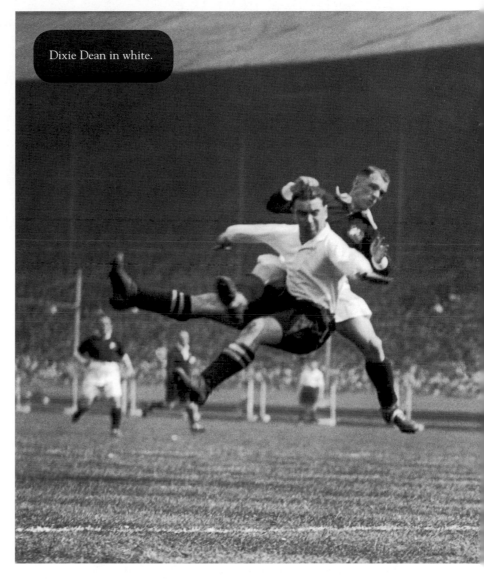

Dixie Dean in white.

At last it is over. The curtain dropped on Saturday on a League campaign that has never been equalled for the intensity of its struggles or the dramatic character of its close.

And in a season of wonderful performances there has been nothing quite comparable to Sheffield Wednesday's magnificent fight for safety. Two months ago their doom seemed sealed. To save themselves, it was necessary to achieve something as strange as fiction.

Yet they did it. They passed undefeated through their last ten games, and actually won seventeen of the twenty points at stake in their matches.

From being the playthings of fate they became one of the most formidable of combinations, and the last day of the season found them so far recovered that one point in their final match meant League safety.

They went one better than this, and got both the points at stake in spite of a fine display by Olney in the Aston Villa goal. Swiftly directed Wednesday attacks were repelled time and again in the first half, but early in the second the Hillsborough team got the all-important first goal.

Jimmy Seed whose departure will now more than ever be mourned by Spurs followers, made the opening, and another ex-London player, Jack Allen, last season with Brentford, put the ball in. That made the issue safe; Trotter's second goal merely emphasised their success.

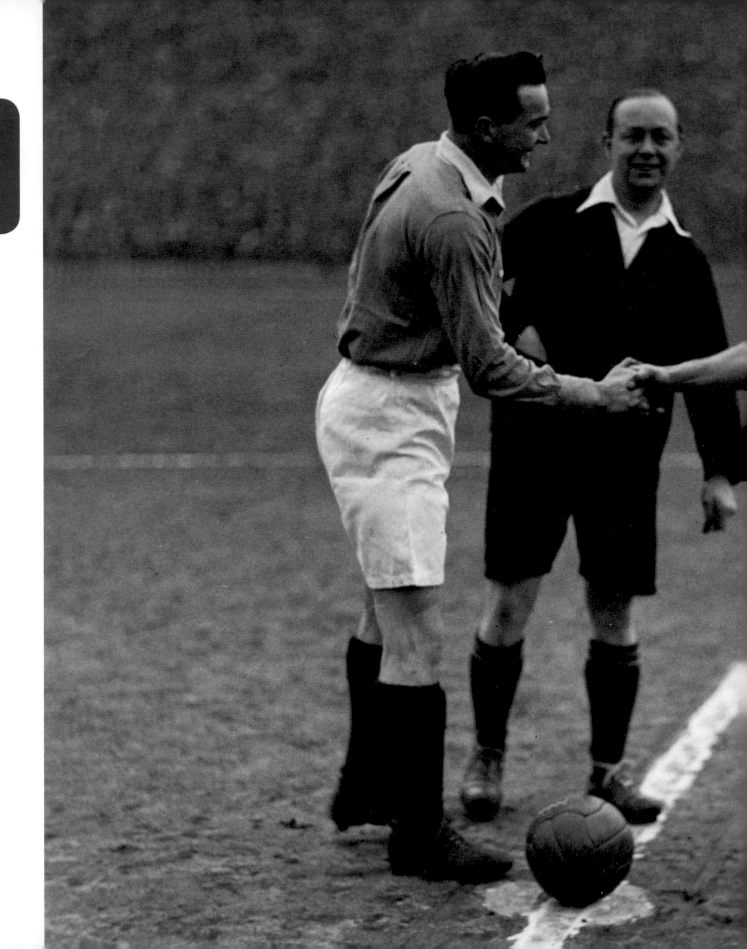

FA Cup.
Manchester
United 1-0
Birmingham City,
18 February 1928.
Captains Wilson
and Bradford.

On Saturday morning Manchester United were at the foot of the League table and a worse goal average than any of their companions in distress. But they set about the strength of Liverpool in a whole-hearted fashion, ran up four goals in the first half and added two more in the second.

THREE FOR SPENCE

Spence got three goals for the winners, Rawlings two and Hanson the other.

Sunderland, whose proud boast it is that they have never been in the Second Division, saved themselves at the expense of their neighbours, Middlesbrough.

The coup de grace was administered on the Middlesbrough ground, so that there was even more merit than would otherwise have been the case in the Wearsiders' performance.

Middlesbrough had the better of the first half, but a mistake by their backs let Wright through. The thrustful Halliday got a second goal after the change of ends, and Middlesbrough unluckily fell further behind when one of their own players deflected the ball into his own net. No wonder the Ayresome men finished the game in a dejected mood.

And so it comes about that Middlesbrough and the Spurs become associated companions in distress. They are both clubs with big resources, and one can but wish them luck in fighting their way back to the Premier Division, but that is no easy task, as Chelsea, Preston, West Bromwich Albion, the Wolves, the Nottingham clubs and others have discovered.

POSTSCRIPT

The final day agony for Middlesbrough and Spurs came amid the tightest points spread in Football League history. Seven teams finished above Spurs by just one point; fourth-place Derby finished just seven points better off than bottom-placed Boro.

For champions Everton, their prolific goalscorer Dixie Dean scored a record sixty league goals.

The First Time Numbers were worn on Players' Shirts

SWANS AT CHELSEA

WELSHMEN BEATEN BY FOUR GOALS

Chelsea 4 Swansea 0

Chelsea outplayed Swansea for most of the match at Stamford Bridge, and won by four clear goals. Elliot scored the only goal of the first half. But others were added through Crawford, Pearson and Biswell after the change round.

Chelsea's form was most encouraging, and Elliot was a great success at centre-forward. But Chelsea's chief strength was at half-back, where Irving, Townrow and Bishop made a magnificent line that kept Swansea's speedy forwards in almost complete subjection.

BRILLIANCE OF BROWN

WEDNESDAY GOALKEEPER'S FINE WORK AGAINST THE ARSENAL

Sheffield Wednesday 3 Arsenal 2

The Wednesday got off the mark better yesterday than they did a season ago, and Arsenal had to admit defeat at Hillsborough by the odd goal of five.

Arsenal, who wore distinguishing numbers, played good football, and probably owe their defeat to the brilliance of Brown, the Wednesday keeper, who made some remarkable clearances in the closing stages of a fast game.

Jones drew first blood for Arsenal, but Hooper equalised just before the interval from a penalty. Brain again gave the Londoners the lead in the second half, but Marsden levelled matters direct from a free kick, and Hooper scored the winning goal.

Arsenal players Alf Baker, Billy Blyth and Jimmy Brain.

1930 Monday 21st April

The First 6-6 Draw in the Football League

12 GOALS AT LEICESTER

Leicester 6 Arsenal 6

Leicester City and the Arsenal, who have met twice during the holiday, have drawn each time. Their meeting at Filbert Street yesterday produced twelve goals.

The scorers were:- Adcock (two), Lochhead, Hine, Harry and Chandler for Leicester, and Bastin (two) and Halliday (four) for the Arsenal.

Five days after drawing with Leicester, Arsenal (below) beat Huddersfield Town 2-0 to win the FA Cup. Two days after the FA Cup final, Arsenal lost 0-1 at home to Sunderland. And now they complain of too many matches in a week!

The First Time a London Team Wins the League

HIGHBURY TRIUMPH

ARSENAL BRING THE LEAGUE FLAG SOUTH AT LAST

Arsenal 3 Liverpool 1

P.J. Moss

The Arsenal have at last won the League. They beat Liverpool at Highbury yesterday 3-1, and that landed them high, and dry above the possibilities of any other club.

The championship has never come south of Birmingham since it was instituted in 1888-89. Bristol City were second in 1907, the Spurs second in 1921-22, Cardiff second in 1923-24 and the Arsenal second in 1925-26.

That was the first record put up by the Arsenal. The second is that they have already scored more points than any other side winning the title. West Bromwich had sixty in 1919-20 and Liverpool sixty in 1922-23, The Arsenal's in what been the result of consistency.

Yesterday's match with Liverpool was a splendid exhibition. Both teams played fast, skilful football. Liverpool were best at the start, the Arsenal outstayed them, and in the end were good winners.

NO MAD STAMPEDE

There was plenty of cheering from the 45,000 spectators at the finish, but there was no mad stampede across the pitch. The Arsenal railings are not too easy to climb, but I thought the crowd took the success quite calmly.

Liverpool, as I have said, started with great dash. They had a strong wind behind them and for a time nearly all the play was in the Arsenal lines.

Liverpool were in front after three minutes. After several

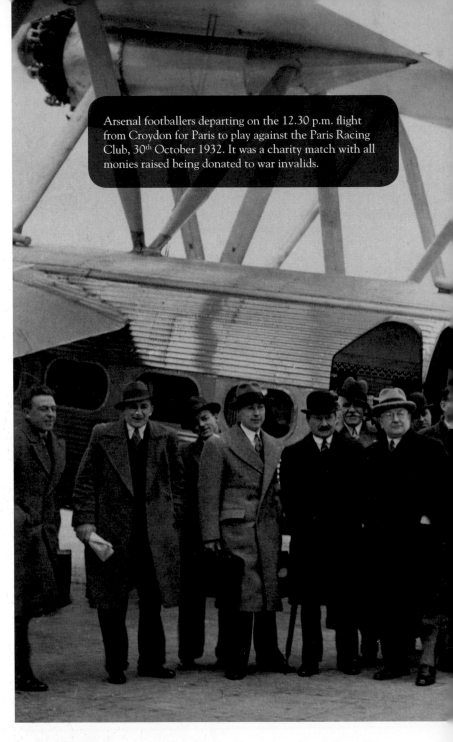

Arsenal footballers departing on the 12.30 p.m. flight from Croydon for Paris to play against the Paris Racing Club, 30ᵗʰ October 1932. It was a charity match with all monies raised being donated to war invalids.

and it beat him.

For a time the Arsenal were outplayed, although Lambert had one fine chance of equalising. Then Barton, brought off a similar effort, but this time Parker cleared, and Hodgson missed, at close range from a nice pass by Gunson.

Arsenal gradually found their game. Bastin hit the underpart of the crossbar with a rasping shot, and Lambert shaved the bar with another.

Half-way through, from a corner kick well taken by Bastin, Jones dropped the ball into the goalmouth and Jack equalised.

BRILLIANT ATTACK AND DEFENCE

Hulme and James played some brilliant football up to the interval, but there was no more scoring, the back play on both sides being splendid, Parker and Jackson standing-out from their respective sides.

It was the Arsenal's game in the second half, although Liverpool were always dangerous in their raids.

Bastin put them in front after twenty minutes. Lucas handled and, following the free kick, James flicked the ball to Bastin, who cut in and scored cleverly.

Some clever work by Lambert gave Hulme a chance to send in a perfect centre. Lambert was there to take the return pass and score a copybook goal.

The Liverpool defence tired under the pressure towards the close, but it held out and, indeed, Liverpool nearly scored in the last minute. With Harper out of his goal the ball bobbed about in the goalmouth, but the back scrambled it away.

It was as good a game as I have seen fit at Highbury this year, and there was real Cup-tie excitement as thrill followed thrill in the exciting exchanges.

raids on the Arsenal goal, Barton, the outside-right, flashed in a fine low centre bang at the Arsenal goal. Roberts tried to kick it out but the ball hit him on the leg and screwed off wide of Harper's left hand.

He had positioned himself to take the shot and had no chance after it struck Roberts. One could not blame the Arsenal pivot. He had to take a very awkward kick at a very fast ball,

Football League Division One	
Arsenal... 3	**Liverpool... 1**
Jack	Roberts (o.g.)
Bastin	
Lambert	

1931 Saturday 25th April

The Most Ever Goals Scored in a Season in the Top Flight – 128

VILLA AND SCORING RECORD

Aston Villa 4 Manchester City 2

When Houghton scored Aston Villa's fourth goal in the match against Manchester City on Saturday he enabled his side to equal the League record score of 128 which Bradford City set up as members of the Northern Section of the Third Division in the 1928-29 season.

The previous best for the First Division was Sheffield Wednesday's total of 105 made last season. As the Villa have yet another match to play – they meet the Wednesday next Saturday at Sheffield – they have a good chance of setting up a new record.

It is worthy remembering that the Villa have scored in every match but two this season, their blank afternoons being in away games with Newcastle and Portsmouth.

POSTSCRIPT

In the event, Villa's 3-0 defeat to Wednesday a week later meant they failed to add to their tally, but the total remains a top-flight record.

Football League Division One	
Aston Villa... ( ) 4	Manchester City... ( ) 2

Chelsea v Aston Villa playing the following season and still scoring goals. Fred Biddlestone the Aston Villa goalkeeper clears from Hughie Gallacher the Chelsea forward during a 6-3 Villa victory at Stamford Bridge.

More used to playing in front of crowds like this at Highbury,
Arsenal were humbled at Walsall.

1933 Saturday 14th January

England's Most Successful Club in
FA Cup Shock

ARSENAL'S AMAZING CRASH

Walsall 2 Arsenal 0

Saturday may have been a dream to the small teams in the Cup-ties, but it was something akin to a nightmare for the "big noises".

Walsall led the way and gave the Arsenal the shock of their lives in defeating them by two goals to none.

The Londoners were completely unsettled and their craft failed against the bustle and energy of the Black Country men.

Jack and James tried desperately hard to set the "machine" going, but always the Arsenal found themselves robbed of the ball.

Alsop, Walsall's leading goalscorer, drove the first nail into Arsenal's coffin and Sheppard, with a penalty, completed the job.

The crowd were almost mad with excitement and the players were carried shoulder high off the field. Thus a struggling Third Division team created a sensation of the century.

FA Cup Third Round	
Walsall... (0) 2	Arsenal... (0) 0
Alsop	
Sheppard	

The Biggest Football League Crowd Outside of Wembley

TRAGIC ERRORS BY STOKE WINGER

KICK AND RUSH TACTICS PULL MANCHESTER CITY THROUGH

Manchester City 1 Stoke City 0

Manchester City passed on to their third semi-final in successive years before a crowd of 84,568 – a ground record for any tie in England except the final – by the aid of kick and rush tactics that have transformed them into the fastest moving attackers in English football.

But what luck they had in the first half. Stoke should have scored from simple openings, in the second and twenty-ninth minutes, yet they wasted what were literally golden opportunities.

In the fourteenth minute Brook, Manchester City's electric left-winger, got the cheapest yet most valuable goal of his career.

He drove a ballooning centre from touchline towards goal, and everyone thought the ball would fall behind. It swerved, however, and John, Stoke's tall goalkeeper, leapt at it, and even when he failed to hold it, it seemed as if he expected it to drop beyond the goal.

CROWD STUNNED

Then it fell just inside the post, and several seconds elapsed before the gigantic crowd realised that the only goal of the match had been scored.

After Stoke's early mistake, which, like the second, lay at the door of Matthews, their nineteen-year-old right-winger, the City's goal practically stunned the crowd.

Both Matthews's chances were obtained through mistakes by someone else. On the first occasion the referee allowed Johnson, Stoke's outside-left, to go on from a position several yards offside, with a linesman flagging.

The second error was committed by Dale, Manchester City's left-back, who missed the centres by Johnson on both occasions.

Matthews was only six yards from goal. First he shot at Dale, who had fallen back, and next time he pulled his shot, and Swift, the home goalkeeper, raced after it and saved.

Manchester City never reached their best except at half-back, where Bray played so well that McLuckie, for whom he deputised, was not missed. Busby, right-half, was the cleverest player on view.

FA Cup Sixth Round	
Manchester City... (1) 1	Stoke City... (0) 0
Brook 14	
	Att: 84,568

THE CUP CROWDS AND CASH IN A NUTSHELL

	Att:	Receipts
Arsenal 1 Aston Villa 2	67,000	£6,366
Bolton Wanderers 0 Portsmouth 3	52,000	£3,778
Manchester City 1 Stoke City 0	84,000	£5,426
Preston North End 0 Leicester City 1	39,000	£3,406

The following month City went on to beat Portsmouth in the FA Cup final at Wembley 2-1.

Most Goals Ever Scored on One Day in the Football League – 209 in 44 games

DEPUTIES DO THE TRICK

LEWIS AND SIMPSON GIVE HAMMERS PEP

West Ham 6 Bury 0

P.J. Moss

West Ham have come into their very best form in exactly the nick of time. They beat Bury at Boleyn Castle by taking their chances.

West Ham's promoted players both had a personal triumph. Lewis scored three times, and Simpson, feeding the wings well, notched one of the points. Lewis will be hard to displace even when Goulden is fit. The ex-Arsenal man was at times the life and soul of the Hammers' attack.

Three goals were scored in each half. Bury gave the crowd a shock in the first minute when Raynor ran right through, and his shot, well wide of Conway, struck Walker and rebounded into play. There was brilliant passing by both sides after this and both goals were threatened before. After six minutes, delightful combination between Marshall, Simpson and Lewis ended with the latter scoring from close in.

Bury took up the attack. West Ham rather foolishly I thought, packed their goal for a time. Matthews was nearly through once and Conway saved a great shot from Buttery. Then, rather against the run of the play, Morton and Marshall worked another fine opening for Lewis who made no mistake

QUICK GOALS

Just on the interval Ruffell put in a good shot from a free kick. Fairhurst punched out and the ball fell at Morton's feet, steadying himself he drove in a shot which gave Fairhurst no chance. The second half was a minute old when Morton worked another opening for Lewis, and again he drove the ball truly out of Fairhurst's reach.

Bury were soon after this a tired, dispirited team, but their goal escaped for a long time. Then Cockcroft, from thirty yards out, drove in a tremendous low ball through a crowd of players. Fairhurst got his hands to it, but it was too heavy to hold.

Bury made many flashes in the second half, but held the ball too close. Conway saved from Graham, Matthews, Buttery and Whitfield before Simpson in the closing minutes scored.

BEES HAVE AN EASY AFTERNOON

Brentford 5 Wolverhampton 0

Brentford up to First Division standard? This result seems to answer the question. Wolves were out-stripped, out-manoeuvred and out-played – or very nearly.

Mathieson, the Brentford goalkeeper, could seldom have had an easier afternoon. The number of shots he had to save could be counted on the fingers. Easy bonus money for Mathieson.

Over-keenness marred the work of both sides early on, but once Brentford had taken the lead – Reid gave it them after twelve minutes – there was never any doubt as to the result.

Shortly before the interval McCulloch headed Brentford's second goal from Reid's centre.

Wolverhampton were dangerous on the resumption and Wrigglesworth had a goal disallowed through offside. Brentford were again superior in attack, and McCulloch headed their third goal from a perfect centre by Reid. Five minutes later Scott added a fourth after more good work by Reid.

Holliday scored a fifth goal for Brentford, who, superior in practically all departments, won as easily as the five goals make out.

POSTSCRIPT

West Ham's and Brentford's victories came on a remarkable day. With 209 goals in forty-four games, this was the most prolific set of results in English football history. Highest scorers were Chester with a round dozen, thanks to a 12-0 thrashing of York.

In the days before all-seater grounds, a typical 1930s terrace.

41

A Record 10 Goals in a Game

HE SCORED ALL THESE

WAS CONGRATULATED BY GOALIE

Luton Town 12 Bristol Rovers 0

After Joe Payne, Luton Town footballer, had scored ten goals in a game yesterday and set up a new record for the Football League, the first man to congratulate him was the goalkeeper who had let the goals through.

Payne has played full-back, half-back and in four positions in the reserve forward line.

Yesterday, making only his fourth appearance in first-class football he got his chance at centre-forward.

And Joe Payne took it. Luton's opponents, Bristol Rovers, were beaten 12-0. Originally Payne was credited with nine goals, but after the match the referee said that Luton's sixth goal, which had been given to Martin, belonged to Payne as the ball was already over the line when Martin charged the goalkeeper.

So Payne surpasses the feat of R. Bell now of Everton, who last Boxing Day scored nine goals for Tranmere Rovers in their 13-4 win over Oldham Athletic.

When interviewed yesterday, Payne gave all the credit to his colleagues for the way in which they had supported him. "He was particularly grateful for the congratulations of Ellis, the Bristol Rovers goalkeeper" said a member of his club.

ON THIS DAY

Britain threatened sanctions against Italy for the latter's invasion of Abyssinia... heavy mid-April snow fell on Exmoor... The BBC apologised to the bellringers of St. Peter Mancroft Church, Norwich, for a broadcast of bells of the church which was described by the vicar, as "an extraordinarily poor idea of what the bells are capable of."

Football Division Three (South)

Luton Town... 12	Bristol Rovers... 0
Payne 10	
Martin	
Roberts	

1937 Saturday 1st May

The First Televised Match

SUNDERLAND'S CUP – AND THAT DEFENCE WON IT

Sunderland 3 Preston North End 1

G.W. Chisholm

Team all the Talents? Old Invincibles? Oh, no – Just Sunderland. Just Preston North End. Just a Cup Final, you'll understand. Bit impoverished in the first half. But it came to life afterwards.

Of course, there were wisps of the football that is football, full quota of goals, two peaches, one (as usual) of debatable value – and Sunderland won the Cup. Last mentioned point big enough history. Sunderland's "year" at last.

Was Gurney offside when he scored the equaliser? Preston players said yes. Everybody around me agreed with them.

Queen Elizabeth, watched by King George VI presents the Cup to the Sunderland captain, Raich Carter.

Suspicious? Oh, rather. Corner kick by Burbanks. Preston defenders moved forward. Carter headed towards goal and the ball might have gone in, but Gurney neatly let the ball brush his hair to help it on its way.

And one Preston player – Beattie, I think – was between Gurney and the goal. The white shirt was just wide of the far goalpost. So I make it a good goal.

Well, Sunderland always had the ability to win, but for a long time pretended that they hadn't. Preston took the first half not only by a goal, but by the cooler methods. Not the better team, but the more composed.

Opening half a sandwich. Preston for fifteen minutes, a Sunderland threat of recovery, and Preston again. Second half undoubtedly Sunderland's. They finished in full cry, something like Sunderland and undoubtedly decisive winners.

And right here you have the key to the result, (it was Johnston's mastery of Frank O'Donnell, Preston's too great faith in O'Donnell, McNab's sterling defence first and aggressive attack later, and the escape of Duns and Burbanks from the clutches of the Preston defenders in the second half.

At half-time Sunderland's chances were not rosy. Preston had plodded steadily, yet it wasn't until approaching the interval that the attacks really penetrated to the danger point.

Anyway, they went in with the lead of Frank O'Donnell's grand goal. A master goal. Nifty footwork and passing, outside-right Dougal, from centre-forward position, making the pass to O'Donnell all on his own out on the right.

Preston might have deserved the lead if only because of the art that brought the goal, but level pegging would have done nobody any harm. Mark this, though, hereabouts Preston had their eye in. Another five or ten minutes might have seen Sunderland securely nailed.

Well, you know what happens when the tea interval comes and the batsman is in the nineties. Preston came back after the break and were promptly bowled.

Gurney got that goal in seven minutes. Sunderland withstood an onslaught and then galloped away with it.

Carter, naturally, scored the second. And, naturally, he got it from the inside-left position. That's the Carter way. Just beat

THE NEWCASTLE BREWERIES

The roads were thickly lined by cheering fans as the coach turned from New Bridge Street into the High Street in Sunderland. Raich Carter and Patrick Gallacher guard the FA Cup. Carter was one of six English players in the Sunderland team.

Gallimore to the ball to crown a Gallacher-Gurney move.

Then the goal that ranks with O'Donnell's as a great one. Copybook wingman's goal. Following a throw-down after injury to Gurney, the centre-forward flicked the ball to Gallacher. Out to Burbanks and, with Gallacher inviting a return pass, Burbanks swept in at speed to release a rocket shot.

NEVER TUMBLED IT

Write down Burbanks and Duns as the star forwards and you won't be far wrong. Neat dodges by Gurney, but Carter wasn't Carter. Beattie did well when he stuck to Duns, but as time

went on Duns simply refused to stick to Beattie. Duns seldom failed to get the ball across.

So it would seem that, as expected, this skilful Sunderland attack was the match-winning factor. In the end, yes. In the main, no.

The maligned Sunderland defence did it. They would not be rocked when the game looked like going Preston's way. Gorman very good. But how much was due to Johnston tying up Frank O'Donnell can best be indicated by Preston's undying faith in their centre-forward. He once got free to score, but was never a mainspring in the game And Preston never tumbled to it.

FA Cup Final	
Sunderland... (0) 3	Preston North End... (1) 1
Gurney	O'Donnell
Carter	
Burbanks	
	Att: 93,495

POSTSCRIPT

Of the twenty-two players for this final twelve were Scottish; both managers were also Scottish.

45

The Russians Are Coming

DYNAMO CROWD BREAK INTO HOUSES

Chelsea 3 Dynamo Moscow 3

Soccer fans who failed to get in to see the Chelsea v Moscow Dynamo game at Stamford Bridge yesterday broke down the doors of nearby houses and ran upstairs in the hope of seeing the game from the roof.

Police threw them out. A hundred thousand people fought for a view of the game.

Extra police rushed to the ground were swept aside as thousands of cheering fans rushed the staff entrance and swarmed into the ground.

This was already crammed to capacity, but the crowd shouldered their way through police barriers and under the horses of the mounted squads, and then fought their way on to the top of already over-packed stands.

Others – risking electrocution on the Underground railway line – raced across the rails to take up positions on the other side of the ground. It was easily the ground's biggest crowd.

The oldest gate official at the Chelsea ground, Frank Porter, told me: "I've never seen anything like it.

"A good half of the crowd have not seen a thing, but they've been cheering like men and women possessed every time the whisper has gone back that Chelsea or the Dynamos have made a brilliant pass or a great save."

A mounted officer told me: "There was just nothing we could do. Thousands on top of the stands and those swirling around the outskirts here have got in without paying, but they're in the same boat as many who have paid to get in. They didn't see anything."

Those who did see the game gasped when the Russians appeared with red and white bouquets and courteously handed them to their Chelsea opposite numbers on the field.

Friendly	
Chelsea… (2) 3	**Dynamo Moscow… (0) 3**
Goulden	Kartsev
Williams	Archangelskiy
Lawton	Bobrov
	Att: 85,000

POSTSCRIPT

For a nation battered and almost bankrupted by war, and with the population facing years of austerity, football provided blessed light relief. With the ending of hostilities, crowds flooded back to grounds, and the 1945 tour of Dynamo Moscow caused a sensation, despite the rather mean-spirited official hospitality extended to the visitors, in an early sign of Cold War tensions. A week after this match, Dynamo beat Arsenal 4-3 at White Hart Lane.

Standing room only!

ENCLOSURE 9D STANDING ONLY

BE... OF PICKPOCKETS

ENCLOSURE STANDING ONLY

47

Newcastle Hand Out a 13-0 Thrashing

SHACKLETON'S FIVE-GOAL DIVIDEND

Newcastle 13 Newport County 0

Stanley Russell

Overshadowing even the threat of a strike on October 15th was yesterday's sensational Newcastle debut of Len Shackleton, who scored five of his side's thirteen goals against unhappy Newport County, three in six minutes.

It isn't every player who can cut a big transfer fee down to a thousand pounds a goal in his first match, so Len, and Newcastle, will be feeling very pleased with themselves this morning.

But the feat will not be such good reading for at least three managers in the London area. Charlton's Jimmy Seed was smothered under the storm of pound notes that changed hands for Shackleton.

But two of his not-so-distant colleagues will be sorry they made such remarks as "He's not worth that number of shillings" when the deal was made.

My best spy reports that the Newport County goalkeeper, Turner, is organising a strike of all goalkeepers against Mr Shackleton.

Football League Division Two

Newcastle... 13	Newport County... (0) 0
Shackleton 5	
Wayman 4	
Milburn 2	
Bentley	
Wookey (o.g.)	

Len Shackleton.

49

Sir Matt Busby's First League Title Win

WONDERFUL UNITED!

ARSENAL CRASH TO THE TEAM OF YEAR

Manchester United 6 Arsenal 1

Stan Halsey

What a whopping Manchester United gave Arsenal! There was only one team in it at any time – and United, worthy champions, pulled no punches.

Manchester United showed that they thought the only proper way to celebrate winning the League championship was to shatter Arsenal, the Cup final hope of the South, and they proceeded to do it.

United started with a spell of sparring Soccer, subtly seeking the opening to land a goal punch. Behind it was Johnny Carey captain and right-half, undoubtedly one of the greater Soccer strategists of our day. What manager Matt Busby is to United off the pitch, Carey is to them on it.

It was Carey who had the Arsenal defence fumbling in the seventh minute. From thirty yards he sent over a cunning lob. It was a hint to Pearson to challenge centre-half Shaw so that the ball rolled to Rowley. Wham! It was in the net.

Centre-half Shaw in the thirtieth minute was hit by a hard ball which winded him and in falling he sustained a suspected fracture of the left wrist.

Then with Forbes lying hurt, play swept down on a wave of United attack. Pearson took a perfect pass from Downie, sold the dummy twice, catching Swindin on the wrong foot the second time to score a brilliant second goal for United. Byrne, on the crest of more fascinating football, made it 3-0 at half-time!

In the second half Manchester United played with a sense of their mission accomplished. Many moves that would have been powerful goal thrusts earlier became playful cuffs.

Even so, United scored three more goals. They couldn't help it. The instinctive football in Johnny Carey could not resist making the pass that sent Rowley smartly through for United's fourth goal.

Roper fouled Downie and conceded a penalty, from which Rowley scored an emphatic goal.

Roper, hurt by a kick, left the field in the second half. Pearson, who with an almost magic touch contrives to turn the penalty box into a danger zone, scored United's sixth goal, while Freddie Cox managed a consolation.

John Carey, Manchester United captain leads his team off the pitch.

Football League Division One

Manchester United ... 6	Arsenal... 1
Rowley (3)	Cox
Pearson (2)	
Byrne	

Matt Busby during his playing days for Liverpool in 1934.

1952 Saturday 3rd May

Only Seven Fit Arsenal Players End the Match

A REAL CAPTAIN'S TRIBUTE

38-YEAR-OLD JOE MERCER WILL PLAY FOR ARSENAL NEXT SEASON

Newcastle 1 Arsenal 0

Stan Halsey

What a tribute to a beaten Cup final side. Arsenal's thirty-eight-year-old captain, Joe Mercer, was so warmed by the reception accorded him yesterday, he has decided to play on for another season.

Joe doesn't have to play soccer. He's well-established in business but I think I know his feelings for his team-mates after being crushed in the last six minutes and with only ten men on the field.

Walley Barnes, Arsenal right-back in peak form, was injured in the early minutes of the game. An innocent back-heel by Milburn caught Walley's knee instead of the ball.

Barnes played on gamely – then went off for treatment. He returned, tried a few limping moves on the left-wing then in the thirty-fifth minute left the field for good.

Don Roper, Arsenal's powerful left-winger, had to desert attack for defence as deputy for Barnes. He suffered his

heartbreak moment, too.

Hoping to break up a menacing move, he went up for the ball with Milburn. He fell, sprawled on the ground and helplessly watched Mitchell, the Newcastle mischief-maker left-winger, collect and cross the ball to George Robledo's head.

George sensed that here was the moment of triumph. He placed the ball with a short sharp header wide of goalkeeper Swindin. It glanced from the right-hand post to the net.

So ended a fine Arsenal fight which stretched their courage and resources to the limit. One bitter moment and soccer's supreme trophy lost after they had been the more commanding side up to the time of Barnes's exit.

It is my view, however, that the Barnes disaster reacted against Newcastle as well as Arsenal. Coping with a ten-man strategy seemed to upset their out-of-tune efforts to find the famous Newcastle rhythm.

A tendency to dazzle-dribble, beat one man too many, hold the ball too long, cost Newcastle possible goals earlier in the game.

It was a sharp comment on left-winger Mitchell that Newcastle's victory goal came from one of the too few occasions when he crossed the ball direct.

Yet Mitchell proved a bigger menace than centre-forward Jack Milburn.

Milburn seldom escaped the close-up, vigilant marking of Ray Daniel. Arsenal's pivot, who had his left arm in a plastic bandage.

An even bigger Newcastle disappointment was Foulkes, inside-right. He did not begin to play till moved to the wing.

Daniel despite his sore arm had a splendid game. So did Forbes, Arsenal right-half, and Joe Mercer on his left.

Forbes strained every atom of energy in endeavouring to make the power of ten men match that of eleven. Joe Mercer was a splendid blend of leadership and action.

Their performances shone out in this valiant Arsenal effort.

Arsenal's gameness assured a few bright bits of football – but not enough. The tricky pitch made it necessary to watch the ball warily all the time.

Arsenal strove for an early goal. In the fourth minute they

nearly got one. Centre-forward Cliff Holton with a long throw-in caught the Newcastle defence in a flap.

Lishman, playing well at that time, tried an adventurous overhead kick. Luck, not judgement, saved goalkeeper Simpson. The ball went narrowly outside.

Holton started by bothering Brennan, Newcastle's centre-half, quite a bit. His play got increasingly clueless against Brennan's experience and he shifted out to the wing.

Logie, in pain from the injury which made him doubtful almost to the kick-off, played courageously. Cox tried hard.

But the attack was not effective enough to overwhelm players like McMichael, Newcastle's brilliant left-back, who scored a personal triumph.

To George Robledo went the sweetness of the victory moment, yet I think his brother Ted, at left-half, however, stole the family football honours.

FA Cup Final

Newcastle... (0) 1	Arsenal... (0) 0
Robledo	
	Att: 100,000

POSTSCRIPT

Arsenal's brave performance is put into starker relief by the fact that by the time the match ended, the side had only seven, perhaps even six, fit players. Barnes had been taken off while Daniel, Horton, Logie and Roper all came into the game carrying injuries or picked up knocks during it.

The Matthews Final

DRAMATIC FINISH BY BLACKPOOL

Blackpool 4 Bolton 3

Stan Halsey

A dramatic storming finish with three goals in the last fifteen minutes gave Blackpool the FA Cup at Wembley – the greatest fighting Cup victory since the war.

Farm struck the most disastrous moment of his career one and a half minutes, after the start.

He fumbled and failed in that nervy opening spell when Bolton scored. It hit Blackpool with the stunning effect of a k.o. punch, for, as always at Wembley on such an occasion, the side's confidence was shattered.

In fact, Blackpool's fidgety football for the rest of the half showed how badly they had been shaken.

That vital first goal came this way. After ninety seconds of probing play Nat Lofthouse, Bolton's energetic leader and ever-alert chaser of chances pounced on the ball and sent it out to right-winger Holden.

Holden skilfully held the ball, drew the defence, and sent it back to Nat, who was lucky to net this second chance.

The Blackpool marking was none too slick, but Lofthouse hooked the ball from about fifteen yards range.

Farm reached for it, but the ball spun away from his grasping right hand and rolled into the net.

A gift goal. A bonus for Bolton.

Strange are the twists of soccer fortunes. Two weeks ago at Wembley George Farm was one of the heroes of the Scottish side which drew with England.

Bolton's second gift goal came in the fortieth minute after Blackpool had managed to equalise through Mortensen five minutes earlier. Bolton staged a raid and Langton, left-winger manoeuvring inside, crossed the ball from Holden.

Farm ought to have grabbed clear of danger, but skipper Moir's sudden dart at the ball put Farm off completely.

A flick of Moir's head completed the defensive chaos and sent the ball into the net.

Stan Matthews did his utmost to rally Blackpool's hopes.

Mortensen had earlier left the field behind him with a dash full of the fire and fierceness of Mortensen at his best.

His hard cross shot seemed to ricochet from Hassall, Bolton inside-left, helping the defence, before entering the net.

Taylor missed a great opportunity to make it two all. He hit the ball "blind" over the bar.

The injured half-back Bell, playing on the wing, headed through Holden's cross after fifty-six minutes to make it 3-1.

Eleven minutes later from a Matthews inspired move Mortensen cut the lead to boot the ball in from Matthews' centre.

In a storming finish Mortensen put the scores level three minutes from time, and then came Perry's winner in the last minute.

WHAT A FINISH!

Stan Matthews has thus got his Cup winner's medal at last. And how deeply he deserved the honour, which has so long eluded him.

The game never reached greatness, but for excitement it can hardly be surpassed for a long time.

FA Cup Final

Blackpool... ( ) 4	Bolton... ( ) 3
Mortensen 35, 67, 89	Lofthouse 2
Perry 90	Moir 40
	Bell 56

Stanley Matthews (right).

England Humiliated on Home Soil

THE THREE GOALS THAT BROKE ENGLAND'S HEART

England 3 Hungary 6

Bob Ferrier

England's record, unbeaten at home in ninety years of football, was shattered yesterday.

It went to a glorious team from Hungary, a team of fire and fury and imagination and technical brilliance. The equal of anything in the world, a team the like of which has not been seen in this country.

Search out no England man to blame. We had no answer to the extravagance of Hungary's attacking ideas, to the surpassing skill of each individual and to a team which in every phase of the game overwhelmed us.

Never have England lived through such a first half, in all their international history! The Hungarians stunned them in the very first minute with an immaculate goal.

Centre-forward Hidegkuti took a pass from Bozsik, right-half, toppled the England defence with a beautiful swerve and shot a smash from twelve yards high over Merrick's head for a baffling goal.

After eleven minutes the Hungarians hit another. Hidegkuti again scoring from Puskas's pass. Dutch referee Horn said "offside" and Puskas, the "Galloping Major" hid his face in his hands in disgust.

It seemed to be a bad decision. But after fifteen minutes Harry Johnston got England into the game. He intercepted a ball from the scoring boots of Kocsis, swept sixty yards upfield, parted to Mortensen.

The centre-forward beat the claret red defence with the pass, and there was Sewell running on to make it 1-1.

But the Hungarians rose to the challenge and after twenty minutes had gone they turned on seven minutes of soccer such as this stadium has seldom seen and which brought them three more goals. This spell broke England's heart.

First a glorious left-wing Puskas-Czibor movement gave Hidegkuti the second, the shot going in oft Eckersley.

Next Puskas beat Ramsey by simply trailing the ball back with his foot and shooting a goal from a ridiculous angle.

Then right-half Bozsik took a free kick, Puskas rather aimlessly diverted it and in it went at the far post. Where Merrick was I'll never know.

DOGGED RUN

Hungary were leading 4-1, with England beaten into the ground. But when the crowd cheered they found a reserve of strength. Mortensen got through on a rather lucky dogged run to make it 4-2.

The crowd rose to England in the second half to urge them on to a fighting victory. It was not to come. Mortensen was immediately injured.

ATOMIC MAGYARS

Wright was also injured and on swept England's substitutes Hassall, Williams and Kennedy to render aid.

They eventually restarted and it brought another atomic burst from the Magyars. Kocsis headed a Puskas cross against a post, out went the rebound to Bozsik, and from twenty yards both Ramsey and Merrick on the line were completely beaten.

Three minutes later yet another delightful Puskas lob and it was 6-2 against England.

The brilliance of the Hungarian passing had blinded and gagged this England team. Ramsey scored from a penalty after an hour's play but we could hardly hope for four more to win the match.

POSTSCRIPT

This was arguably the defining game in English post-war football – a vivid illustration of how the country that gave the game to the world had been left behind by the tactical innovation and individual brilliance of foreign opponents. The "Atomic Magyars" as the *Mirror* memorably called the Hungarians would soon become known as the "Magical Magyars", but whatever the epithet, the gulf in class was clear, with Hidegkuti operating as a deep-lying centre-forward to utterly confuse England with their rigid and dated "W M" formation.

The defender so embarrassingly exposed for Puskas's first was actually Billy Wright, but Bob Ferrier could be excused for the mistaken identity, so bewildering was Hungary's movement and class.

International	
England... (2) 3	**Hungary... (4) 6**
Sewell	Hidegkuti 3
Mortensen	Puskas 2
Ramsey (pen)	Bozsik

Gilbert Merrick cannot prevent Hungary scoring... again.

The First League Game Played Entirely Under Floodlights

BLACKOUT – SO POLICE BLACKOUT FANS

Portsmouth 0 Newcastle 2

Tony Horstead

History was almost NOT made at Portsmouth last night.

Half an hour before the kick-off time of this first League game ever to be played under floodlights, all the lights went off – except the floodlights.

The entrances, stands, terraces and offices were blacked out because a fuse blew – and this is what happened:

Spectators and officials stumbled, groped and jostled about as they lost their way in the dark.

Police refused to allow any more fans through the turnstiles.

The auxiliary diesel power system was found to be frozen.

Portsmouth and Newcastle players changed by candlelight in the dressing rooms.

OFFICIAL INQUIRY?

Five minutes before the scheduled start at 7 p.m. electricians found the fault outside the ground. The gates were re-opened and the game began eight minutes late.

I understand that the police are to ask for an Official Inquiry.

They want to know why the auxiliary plant was not tested beforehand. As for the game, it was played at a fantastic pace in a biting east wind. The players dashed about so energetically with normal positions forgotten, more through the thought of self-preservation than enthusiasm.

If they had stayed still they would have frozen into statues.

But at least the game gave the 15,000 who braved the cold, thrills and excitement.

It also proved that in normal conditions floodlighting will be a money-spinner. This confident Newcastle side, full of cut and thrust, deservedly took two points because they proved that all the football frills in the world do not equal goals.

Pompey produced pretty, attractive football but never looked dangerous. Newcastle's long passes to the wings and hard crosses to untiring centre-forward Vic Keeble, paid off in the thirty-first minute.

THIRTY YARDER

Keeble chased half a chance, beat goalkeeper Uprichard to the ball and flicked it to Bill Curry, who slammed it into the net.

In the second half Pompey added bite and punch to their delightful approach work.

They pressed continuously and the Newcastle defence were clearing desperately. Still the shooting, however, was anywhere – BUT AT THE GOAL.

The only time Newcastle goalkeeper Simpson was really tested was by a thirty-yard free kick from full-back Mansell.

Then Newcastle broke away with one idea in mind – the shortest route to goal.

Davies pushed the ball to Curry, who raced down the right-wing to the by-line, hooked the ball into the goalmouth and there was Keeble to slam in number two.

And that, justifiably so, was that.

Football League Division	
Portsmouth… (0) 0	Newcastle Utd… (1) 2
	Curry
	Keeble

Goalkeeper Dislocates Five Vertebrae in the FA Cup Final and Plays On

OLD CROCKS RUN OFF WITH THE CUP

REVIE THE SCHEMER. HAYES THE THRUSTER. DYSON THE SURPRISE

Bert Trautmann shakes hands with Prince Philip before the 1956 FA Cup final.

Manchester City 3 Birmingham City 1

Stan Heys

Oh, what a wonderful Manchester double. United carried off the League championship and now City have deservedly run off with the Cup.

Some people called Manchester City the team of "old crocks" because of their many injured men. Those folk must be wearing a rather lop-sided smile this morning.

Not until eleven o'clock on the morning of this match did Manchester manager Les McDowall finally select his team. All week the Manchester camp had been alive with rumours of injuries.

Then Spurdle a developed a painful boil under the arm, and

McDowall's team problem was solved. Revie came into the centre and Johnstone played outside-right.

Bill Leivers, right-back, and Bobby Johnstone both had a shot of novocaine just before the game to dull the pain in injured legs.

Roy Clarke, left-winger, played with a displaced bone in his right leg. At one point in the game it came out of joint again and he had to pause in his play to put it back in himself!

It was Don Revie's experience of Wembley last year which came to Manchester's aid yesterday. He realised that to rush about all over the place is not good on the Wembley turf.

So Manchester used the open spaces. They made Birmingham chase them and in trying to do so they chased themselves out of the Cup. At the end, the Kinsey-Browne-Murphy inside-forward trio looked the most forlorn footballers on the field. They were completely done.

FA Cup Final

Manchester City... (1) 3   Birmingham City... (1) 1

Hayes 3   Kinsey 15
Dyson 65
Johnstone 68

Att: 100,000

Manchester City took the lead in three minutes. A master move brought the goal.

Leivers sent the ball across to Revie who crossed it to Clarke. Then Revie called for a quick return square pass, stepped over the ball and, hey presto, there was Hayes to hit it to the net.

Birmingham were badly jolted by that early shock. Centre-half Smith steadied them up, however, and in the fifteenth minute Kinsey and Brown engaged in a duet which, baffled the Manchester defence and Kinsey scored the equaliser.

The heartening effect of that goal inspired Birmingham to their best spell in the game. They reached a standard of football which indicated they might yet beat Manchester.

But Manchester's tactics gradually brought them the ascendancy. And that brief, bright bit of Birmingham spirit flickered out.

Dyson, with his tendency to dally where direct action is needed, was the player everyone expected would prove the big flop of the forward line.

But in the twentieth second-half minute with the score 1-1, and both teams sweating and fidgeting after the vital lead goal which might so easily mean victory, it was Jack Dyson who rose to the crisis and scored.

A little earlier he tried a snapshot which Birmingham back Jeff Hall cleared from the line. Then came a brilliant pass from Revie – one of the many sparkling football touches with which he celebrated his return to Wembley.

Dyson did not fail. His shot went true into the net.

Three minutes later Dyson the scorer became Dyson the goalmaker. This time he steadied a long ball, stabbed it accurately over to Bobby Johnstone, emergency right-winger, who sent Birmingham sagging into the depths of Cup despair with a coolly-taken goal.

The last fifteen minutes were rough and tough for goalkeeper Bert Trautmann. He ricked his neck when coping with a tackle by Murphy and was shaken again when he collided with Ewing, his own centre-half.

It was Ewing's tactics of following the centre-forward to the wings, while the backs and half-backs covered the front of goal gap he left.

This completely broke the effectiveness of Birmingham's Eddie Brown's movement.

After the match, Cup-winning captain Roy Paul, the froth of celebration champagne still on his lips, said "We'll have another go at the Cup next year. Expect us back at Wembley."

Paul agreed that Manchester City had dictated the pace of the play with a purpose. "It was the result of our experience last year, when we ran ourselves to death with ten men.

"It's no good running with the ball at Wembley. It takes too much out of you. So if the play looked a bit slow – that's the reason. We wanted it that way."

POSTSCRIPT

Trautmann's "ricked" neck proved to be rather more serious. The former German prisoner-of-war actually dislocated five vertebrae, fracturing one!

1957 Wednesday 15th May

Stanley Matthews' Last Game for England aged 42

DANES SCARE 4-GOAL ENGLAND

WE'RE THERE – BUT THIS WAS A SHABBY WORLD CUP PERFORMANCE

Denmark 1 England 4

England won their World Cup match against Denmark here all right tonight – but what a scare they had before making sure of victory in the second half.

Forty thousand Danish fans, who had never given their all-amateur side a hope, could hardly believe their eyes when England were one down after twenty-six minutes.

And the goal that scared the pants off England came from John Jensen, a twenty-year-old inside-right making his first international appearance.

England were back in the hunt with a Johnny Haynes goal two minutes later and with three more from Tommy Taylor (2) and John Atyeo, but this was a shabby performance.

But we are almost certain of being in the World Cup Finals in Sweden next year.

64

A week earlier England had played Northern Ireland in a World Cup Qualifying match at Wembley Stadium. Earl Mountbatten is introduced to Stanley Matthews by captain Billy Wright. England won this game 5-1.

A draw against Eire at Dublin in their last qualifying match next Sunday will do the trick. The trouble with England was that while so many players were trying to do a Matthews the veteran himself had a very quiet game.

The Danish fans gave Duncan Edwards a tough time. He was booed for two fouls in the first half, one of which injured the little outside-right Jurgen Hansen.

England only scored the vital second goal when the Danes eased up thinking the referee had stopped play because their centre-half was hurt. The third goal was obtained against ten men, and the fourth against a beaten team almost on their knees through sheer weariness. At their best, midway through the first half, the Danes pulled out three stunning attacks.

First Alan Hodgkinson dived full length to save. Then he hurled himself through the air to turn the ball round the post. But the third time he had no chance against Jensen's piledriver.

Haynes's equaliser was a just reward. Four shots of his had been charged down and he made no mistake with this one.

In the second half I thought we were going to lose. A football sensation looked like breaking before our eyes.

But the amateurs just couldn't keep it up and Tommy Taylor scored the second unchallenged.

THAT WAS THE END. John Atyeo got the third while Hansen was off the field and Taylor bagged the fourth.

You've heard of "Danish Blue." This was English pink. Our players should be blushing.

World Cup Qualifier

Denmark... (1) 1	England... (1) 4
John Jensen 26	Haynes 28
	Taylor 71, 86
	Atyeo 76

POSTSCRIPT

This was Stanley Matthews' final game for England. At forty-two and having played fifty-four times for his country, "The Wizard of the Dribble" kept on playing club football right up to age of fifty in 1965, completing over 700 league games and becoming professional football's first knight of the realm.

Real Madrid Dominate Europe

REAL CHAMPS

Real Madrid 7 Eintracht Frankfurt 3

Bill Holden

Real Madrid quickly showed what makes them the greatest club side in Europe at Hampden Park, Glasgow, last night.

Eintracht, the 5-1 against underdog team in this European Cup final, hit them hard at first trying for a quick goal.

They almost got it when inside-right Lindner smashed in a shot which Spanish keeper Dominguez punched against the bar and was thankful to see spin away to safety.

The 135,000 crowd were behind the Germans who scored first in the nineteenth minute.

Centre-forward Stein switched to the right-wing and crossed a ball which outside-right Kress ran on to first time and hit home.

Then Real Madrid turned on one of the spells of electrically charged soccer which has given them such fantastic supremacy.

Two goals in three minutes put them ahead. Di Stefano scored both. Outside-right Canario gave him a perfect centre, and Di Stefano stretched out a foot to touch into the net and equalise in the twenty-seventh minute.

Then a Canario shot was blocked by German keeper Loy, and centre-forward Di Stefano ran on to the rebound and hit the ball in.

And on the stroke of half-time, Puskas, who had scarcely been in the game, suddenly snapped up a bad clearance and hammered in a brilliant goal from a most difficult angle.

Real Madrid's Ferenc Puskas surrounded by Kilmarnock schoolchildren the day after the game.

In the fifty-fourth minute Puskas ended Eintracht's hopes when he scored from a dubious penalty given for obstruction.

Six minutes later he completed his hat-trick with a header which made the score 5-1, and then he got another one.

Stein scored again for Eintracht but immediately afterwards Di Stefano completed his hat-trick and it was 7-2.

Then Stein scored again.

European Cup Final

Real Madrid… (2) 7	Eintracht Frankfurt… (1) 3
Di Stefano 27, 30, 73	Kress 19
Puskas 46, 54, 60, 71	Stein 72, 75

Att: 135,000

The First League and Cup Double of Modern Era

SPURS CHAMPS!

JONES INJURED – OUT OF SPAIN GAME

Spurs 2 Sheffield Wednesday 1

Bill Holden

The League Championship trophy will be presented to Spurs on Saturday, April 29th. They won the title without doubt by beating their only challengers, Sheffield Wednesday, in a game where tempers became raw and football was often forgotten.

As I type these words pandemonium reigns at White Hart Lane.

Thousands have broken through a cordon of police, and are spilling across the pitch incessantly chanting: "We want Danny."

They won't go homo before they have paid tribute to right-half Danny Blanchflower – the man who has skippered Spurs so elegantly to the championship and given them a great chance of pulling off the Cup and League double, last achieved in 1897.

It's just before 10 p.m. The men in white shirts are climbing self-consciously into the directors' box to acknowledge the crowd.

The crowd yell for a speech. But not one of the Spurs has enough breath left. Instead, they wave, smile – and disappear for a champagne celebration.

But still the song is ringing in our ears: "Glory, Glory – the Spurs go marching on."

Last night's match, though, was less a march than a battle! Because of it, Cliff Jones, wizard of the right-wing, is out of the Welsh team to meet Spain in the World Cup qualifying game at Cardiff tomorrow.

Cliff had two stitches sewn into his right knee at half-time. He told me: "I am driving Terry Medwin down to Cardiff. I don't think I can play and I'm sure Terry will take my place."

Cliff was first injured as he got the ball into the net seconds after the whistle had signalled him offside.

That sparked off a tough, tense, terrific game in which referee Dawes booked Scottish international Dave Mackay and Wednesday right-back Peter Johnson.

Jones was pulled down by right-half Brian Hill in the twenty-sixth minute. Johnson sent sprawling Spurs' tough, titanic left-half Mackay.

Mackay promptly brought down Sheffield's centre-forward Keith Ellis, then toppled inside-left John Fantham.

Left-back Don Megson took the kick and though his shot was blocked, he scored from the rebound.

Then mighty Spurs turned on a burst which won the match. Bobby Smith, idol of England and White Hart Lane, picked up a long pass from left-winger Terry Dyson and broke through the middle.

He beat the defence and crashed in a brilliant shot.

Spurs came again and Les Allen, inside-left, was sent toppling down. Blanchflower took the kick, right across the field, and centre-half Maurice Norman nodded it down.

It was fantasy as Allen, his back to the goal, curled his body in the air, and got a foot to the ball to hook it into the net.

It brought an explosion – not a cheer. It was the glorious goal that clinched the title.

After the break, Spur showed for ten minutes their cool, precise science.

Then the toughness crept back. Smith, once before spoken to by the referee for charging England keeper Ron Springett into the net, crashed into him again twelve minutes from time.

Springett hit the goalpost and collapsed. He was helped

to the touchline, laid on a stretcher and Johnson went in goal.

But after two minutes Springett gallantly returned.

There were five minutes left. Five minutes of tantalising play with both goals threatened... And then the whistle.

Spurs now need three points from their last three games – two at home – to smash Arsenal's all-time record of sixty-six points in one season.

Bill Nicholson, Spurs' manager, says: "I'm very happy about the triumph. Now for that record."

No one at White Hart Lane last night will doubt that they will do it – and the double too.

POSTSCRIPT

This match marked the first stage for the team dubbed "Super Spurs" completing the legendary "double" of League and Cup. With victory over Leicester in the FA Cup final three weeks later, Tottenham became the first team to win the double since Aston Villa in 1897.

Football League Division One	
Spurs... (2) 2	Sheffield Wednesday... (1) 1
Smith	Megson
Allen	
	Att: 61,205

1962 Sunday 10th June

England Lose to the Samba Boys

GOODBYE, WORLD CUP

TRAGIC MISTAKES BY SPRINGETT COST ENGLAND TWO GOALS

Brazil 3 England 1

Frank McGhee

Another World Cup is over for England – after a game that will always be remembered for the tragic mistakes of one Englishman and the dazzling, dynamic brilliance of one Brazilian.

THE ENGLISHMAN: Goalkeeper Ron Springett, because for once his Jungle-quick reflexes deserted him in two vital moments that cost two heartbreaking goals – two razor-sharp slashes across his country's throat.

THE BRAZILIAN: Garrincha, the greatest right-winger in the world, usually marked by three men in this quarter-final, yet always somehow finding that extra yard of pace and that extra inch of room to create havoc.

This blazing genius, known as the "Little Bird" is the man Springett will remember longest – he scored the first and third goals, and made the second.

It was because of him and him alone that the Brazilians trotted a lap of honour at the end, bearing their national flag, while England trooped off down the tunnel leading to nowhere.

We had the only other forward in the match able to stand almost shoulder to shoulder with Garrincha – left-winger Bobby Charlton, always keeping that great full-back Djalma Santos at full stretch.

We had skipper Johnny Haynes fighting and prompting with all his old urgency.

We had Jimmy Greaves and Gerry Hitchens – recalled at the last minute in place of injured Alan Peacock – looking hungrily for scoring chances.

And although Bryan Douglas looked weary and sold out in the closing stages, he could always dredge up the strength for just one more run. That sort of heart and guts characterised the whole defence, too.

There was an early sensation when inside-right Didi limped off in the fourth minute and England piled the pressure on the ten Brazilian survivors.

But Didi returned after treatment and Brazil countered fiercely. Armfield had to scoop a Garrincha shot off the line.

Then Greaves had a great shot tipped over the bar and Flowers thundered a Haynes cross only inches wide.

But in the thirty-first minute Garrincha struck. Unmarked almost on the penalty spot, "Little Bird" soared up for a corner kick and headed a savagely struck goal.

Maurice Norman, the only England defender tall enough to stand any chance of blocking it, was an awestruck spectator.

Within seven minutes England snatched a dramatic equaliser. Haynes floated over a free kick perfectly and Greaves headed it against the bar.

Before any Englishman could groan in disappointment, Hitchens was on the ball and slipping it sweetly into the net.

With Didi and Amarildo limping, Brazil reshuffled their attack in the second half.

The real tragedy of the match came in the fifty-third minute, when I thought Flowers was harshly punished for a tackle. Garrincha hit the free kick from twenty-five yards with such force that the ball bounced off Springett's chest, and Vava nodded it in.

Six minutes later the fantastic Garrincha struck again, this time picking up a loose ball and hitting it through a gap.

He made the shot dip and swerve, but a world-class keeper could and should have spotted and stopped it. Springett's despairing dive was hopelessly late.

Haynes said afterwards: "At half-time I thought we were in with a chance to win. But then we were hit by that unfortunate second goal and we fell away."

POSTSCRIPT

England's best World Cup showing to date ended at the hands of eventual champions Brazil. The game is remembered chiefly for Garrincha's brilliant display, but also for a hilarious incident when a dog strayed onto the pitch in Vina del Mar. Greaves successfully apprehended the animal, but in the process, the dog urinated all over him. Garrincha found this so funny he reportedly adopted the dog as a pet.

World Cup Quarter-final	
Brazil... (1) 3	England... (1) 1
Garrincha 31, 59	Hitchens 38
Vava 53	

The England team waving goodbye at London Airport before their flight to Santiago, Chile to play in the 1962 World Cup Finals. They were all too soon waving goodbye to the Finals.

1963 Wednesday 15th May

First Ever European Trophy for British Side

MADRID MAULED 5-1

GREAVES SPARKS OFF THE GREAT GOAL RIOT

Spurs 5 Atletico Madrid 1

Ken Jones

Super Spurs won the European Cup Winners' Cup here tonight with this five-goal massacre of Madrid – and became the first British club to carry off one of Europe's top soccer trophies.

It was in the tradition of true champions that Spurs came bursting back to write another glorious chapter in their history.

Their League hopes gone, this Cup final at the Feyenoord Stadium was their last bridgehead into Europe next season.

And suddenly a tired team found the extra energy, courage, and, above all, the extra skill that has taken them to the summit of soccer.

The scoreline hides the true value of their performance.

It disguises the very real fact that for fifteen nail-biting minutes in the second half they suddenly seemed to have "gone."

But it does no injustice to a team smarting under the jibes that they were finished as a football force who came back to hit soccer's high spots again.

At times Spurs were superb. Their cool, controlled football was from the mould of their great days.

And after weeks of fumbling in attack the forwards suddenly clicked again.

Remember that Spurs were without powerhouse wing-half Dave Mackay, who was injured.

Remember that four years at the top has sapped their stamina – and we may never see this side playing in big game competition again.

But above all remember the superb skill. The gazelle-like runs of Cliff Jones looking every inch the perfect winger as he demoralised the Atletico defence.

The return to form of goal ace Jimmy Greaves and the comeback of schemer John White.

The storming centre-half play of mighty Maurice Norman and the cheek and courage of little Terry Dyson, playing his best ever game for Spurs.

Their first goal in the sixteenth minute was one I shall never forget. Centre-forward Bobby Smith, unflinching in the face of some rugged tackles by centre-half Griffa, sent Jones bulleting to the right corner flag.

The Welshman's cross was inch perfect and Greaves batted the ball home on the run.

In the thirty-second minute Dyson hooked one back from the by-line and White, with studied calm, cracked the ball into the roof of the net.

The Spaniards needed a quick goal at the start of the second half, and they got it in the forty-sixth minute.

Left-back Ron Henry punched a shot away from under the bar, and left-winger Collar hammered home the penalty kick.

Suddenly Spurs were in trouble. Goalkeeper Bill Brown had to make a desperate kick away save.

And then Henry, playing all of the second half with strained ligaments in his left knee, headed one off the line from inside-left Mendoza.

Spurs needed luck, and they got it in the sixty-ninth minute when Dyson suddenly snatched an amazing goal.

A quick turn took him inside the full-back, and when he hung his cross high under the bar goalkeeper Madinabeyta backhanded the ball into his own net.

Twelve minutes from time the fans were singing "Glory, Glory Hallelujah" as Spurs made it safe when Dyson's cross

was bludgeoned home on the far post by Greaves.

And fittingly it was Dyson who got the fifth three minutes from time with a shot from the edge of the area.

Spurs manager Bill Nicholson said afterwards: "Dyson played better than I have ever seen him. Norman and Marchi were terrific.

"But don't forget it was that third goal – a fluke that clinched it. We started to get the ball again then.

"I am tremendously proud for the players and my club to be the first manager of a British team to win a European title."

Leo Horn, ace Dutch referee, who watched the game, said: "This was the best performance I have ever seen from an English club. Why doesn't your national team play like this?"

Tottenham Hotspur return to London after their win over Atletico Madrid. Front to back are Tony Marchi holding the Cup, Bill Brown, Morris Norman, Bobby Smith, John White, Peter Baker, Jimmy Greaves, Ron Henry and manager Bill Nicholson with thumbs up.

European Cup Winners' Cup Final

Tottenham Hotspur… (2) 5	Atletico Madrid… (0) 1
Greaves 16, 78	Collar 46, (pen)
White 32	
Dyson 69, 87	

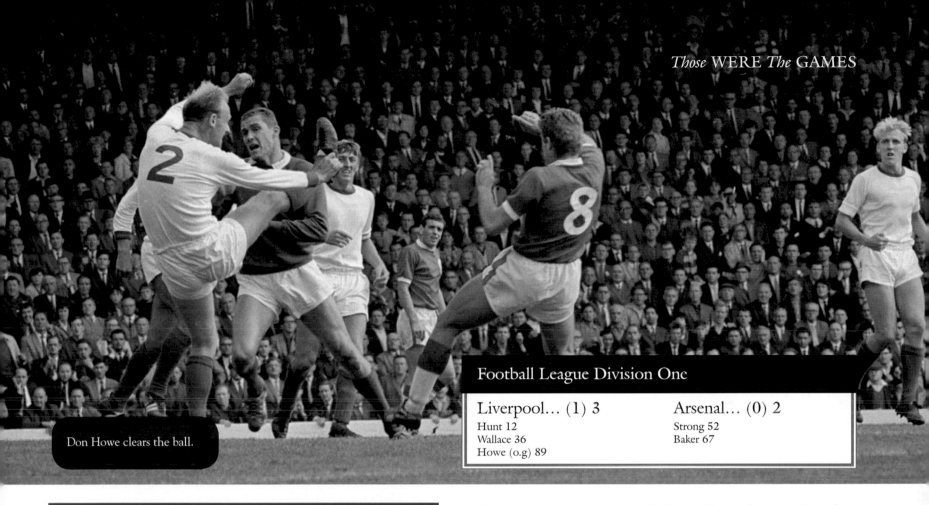

Don Howe clears the ball.

Football League Division One

Liverpool... (1) 3	Arsenal... (0) 2
Hunt 12	Strong 52
Wallace 36	Baker 67
Howe (o.g) 89	

1964 22nd August

First Televised Match of the Day

"I JUST HAD TO GO IN HARD AT HIM, SAYS HOWE."

Liverpool 3 Arsenal 2

Frank McGhee

Don Howe, Arsenal's £45,000 right-back forgot style and elegance. He relied on old-fashioned – and sometimes illegal – methods in his bid to curb Peter Thompson, Liverpool's flying left-winger

After the match Howe – twenty-three caps for England – told me: "I didn't like it, but to me it was necessary. When you're up against a player as good as Thompson is, you can't stand off him.

"You can't let him take the Mickey, he'll murder you. He's the greatest winger. You've got to get in there at him. The crowd don't seem to understand, but it's your job. You've got to do it."

The Anfield Kop crowd were angered and outraged that someone as highly rated as Howe should use such tactics. They singled out Howe as a special target for boos.

From his unhappy second minute when he first sent Thompson crashing to his tormented eighty-ninth minute when he got into the path of a shot from inside-left Gordon Wallace and turned the winning goal far out of Arsenal keeper Jim Furnell's reach.

Howe only got one cheer, when he wrapped a lean arm around Thompson and said, "No hard feelings!" Thompson scissored the Arsenal defence open for Roger Hunt's opening goal in the twelfth minute. Wallace made two with a header.

Fighting Arsenal drew level with goals from Geoff Strong and Joe Baker. They deserved a point.

It was tragic that Howe, the man who had suffered enough, was responsible for denying it.

The First Ever Substitute to be used in a Football League Game

Bolton 4 Charlton 2

Two goals from Bolton winger Francis Lee in the last ten minutes – the first a favour, penalty – were cruel blows to a better side.

Charlton lost goalkeeper Mike Rose with a knee injury after twelve minutes and substitute Keith Peacock came on, with left-back John Hewie taking over in goal.

Bolton took a lucky lead on twenty-one minutes when right-back Billy Bonds headed into his own net in an attempt to clear a centre from Warwick Rimmer, who also scored three minutes later.

Charlton might have been excused had they folded. But new boss Bob Stokoe must be proud of the way his team fought back to equality before half-time with goals from Len Glover and Roy Matthews.

Glover, always a source of worry to right-back Roy Hartle, got magnificent service from seventeen-year-old Alan Campbell at inside-left.

Bolton centre-forward Wyn Davies had a thin time against Frank Haydock.

POSTSCRIPT

Peacock made history by becoming the first substitute in the Football League. He was soon followed by a number of others – and judging by the *Daily Mirror*'s report the reaction was not favourable: "The twelfth men of soccer marched on to the League scene for the first time yesterday – and
how! Thirteen of the new watch-and-play brigade were called into action as managers took advantage of the rule which allows them to replace an injured player.

The crowd at Arsenal jeered Stoke's seventy-ninth-minute stand-in Keith Bebbington. Peterborough's fans booed when Gillingham brought on Ron Newman after seventeen minutes. Said FA chairman Joe Mears: "There were more substitutes than I expected, but for some time, no doubt, clubs will be able to call on a replacement as soon as a man is injured. Eventually, they may find it pays them to wait as long as possible."

Football League Division Two	
Bolton... ( ) 4	Charlton... ( ) 2
Bonds (o.g.)	Glover
Rimmer	Matthews
Lee (2, one pen)	

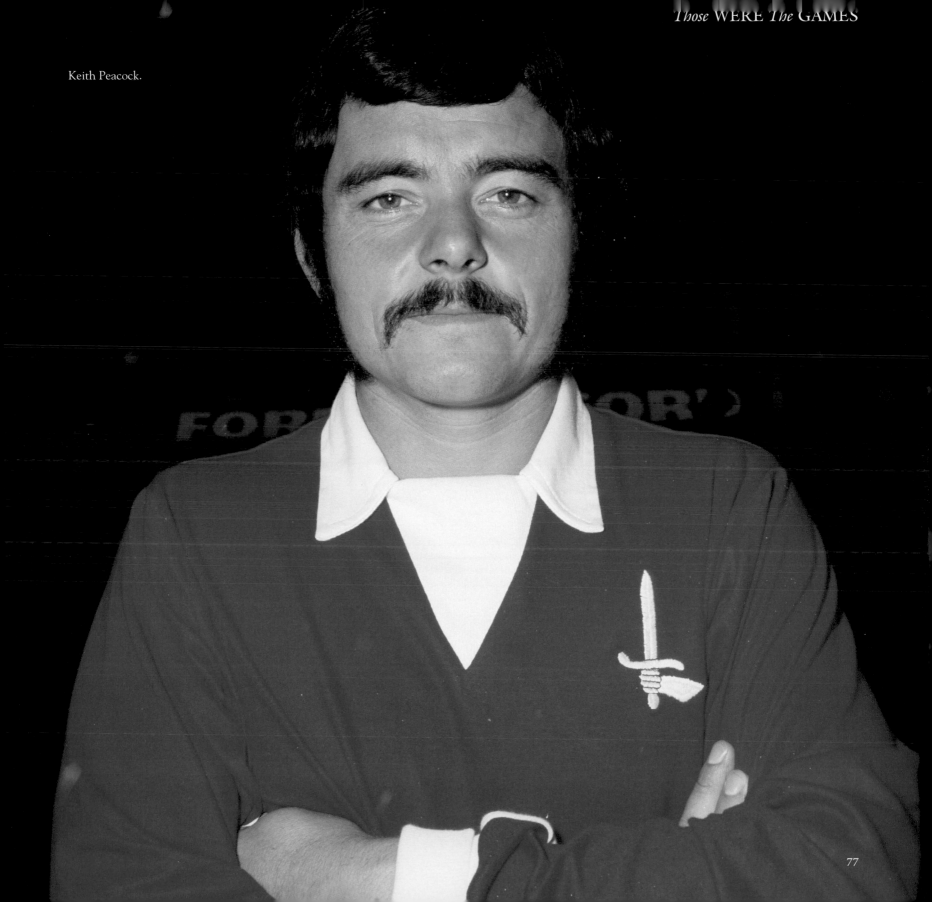

Keith Peacock.

World Cup Final

HAIL THE MASTERS

ENGLAND, THE FOUNDERS OF FOOTBALL, ARE AGAIN ITS MASTERS

England 4 West Germany 2

Sam Leitch

The twelve-inch, Jules Rimet Trophy stays here and the world of football must bow to Alf Ramsey and his English heroes.

What marvellous drama and nail-biting agony accompanied this victory at the £200,000 final. The supreme triumph in England's 103-year-old international span.

It was a fantastic thriller with West Germany equalising fifty seconds from the end of the ninety minutes and forcing the first World Cup final extra time since 1934.

JOY CRAZY

Extra time was stunning with the drama switching to the burly, moustachioed Russian linesman Tofik Bakhramov.

He ruled England had scored her third goal in the 100th minute when referee Gottfried Dienst could not decide about Geoff Hurst's shot against the bar.

Then joy-crazy, flag-waving kids invaded the pitch, with the game not over and with referee Dienst counting off the dying seconds.

There was more to come. West Ham and England inside-left Geoff Hurst scored his third goal and England's fourth with the last kick.

But the memory for me of this Wembley game – not a football classic but 120 thunderous minutes of magnificent sporting emotion – was after the final whistle.

England, their scarlet shirts black with the sweat of this soccer hard labour on a strength-sapping pitch, queued up behind skipper Bobby Moore to touch the gold trophy.

SUPREMACY

How Wembley detonated with its richest roar when Her Majesty the Queen handed Moore, my man of the match, the

Confident German fans.

Cup, emblem of world supremacy wherever a ball is kicked.

Manchester United's Nobby Stiles urged Moore to take the trophy to manager Ramsey, as usual the nonchalant boss.

His straight face hid the emotions he must have felt at attaining the World Championship for which he has worked three years.

SPORTING BUT RAMSEY WOULD NOT TAKE THE TROPHY AND INFRINGE ON THE PLAYERS' MAGIC MOMENT

So Moore led his men on their grand victory lap.

Stiles beckoned the England reserves to follow the sweating, exuberant visitors.

I commend the sporting words of West German team manager Helmut Schoen, who said:

"I think England are real world champions. They had good spirit, tempo and playing ability. It was surely a match which pleased everybody."

It was a masterpiece of sportsmanship. The cheap denigration of the beaten South American contestants was proved totally unfounded by this fast, stirring physical final.

ERROR

First the Germans went ahead because of an English defensive error.

But the tradition of the World Cup final stood out again that the winners always come from behind.

There will be long and passionate debate about the eighty-ninth minute West German equaliser.

England claimed that first Jackie Charlton did not foul for the free kick, then that a German defender handled before Wolfgang Weber stubbed in a close-range shot.

The German fans will argue forever about the third England goal which really broke Helmut Schoen's men.

ROCKET

Had Geoff Hurst's thunderous drive crossed the goal-line when the ball bounced down from the underside of the bar?

The Germans said no and referee Dienst, a forty-six-year-old

post office employee had to consult his linesman who signalled a goal. It was not so much the England goal but the referee consulting the linesman which seemed to shatter the morale of a tiring German team.

Dienst had been a whistle-happy official and I thought he was better placed than his linesman.

But the roar of relief from the many thousands of English throats testified to the tension being felt about this close, clean final.

Helmut Haller got the first West German goal after thirteen minutes when left-back Ray Wilson's header presented the blond German forward with a gift goal.

Wilson, normally one of the safest of England's tight covering defenders, seemed un-nerved at the start because of the dangerous probings of Uwe Seeler, veteran West German centre-forward, who roamed about cunningly on the right-wing for this final.

Hurst's headed equaliser six minutes later came after a quick and cleverly flighted free kick from Bobby Moore.

Moore's captaincy, inspiring drive, positional flare and superlative reading of the match, won him the Football Writers' Association Award of Player of Players.

DYNAMIC

This was a vote taken from the 1,000 world football reporters at the final.

Another West Ham man, runabout Martin Peters, put England ahead in the seventy-seventh minute.

Her Majesty Queen Elizabeth presents the Jules Rimet Trophy to England captain Bobby Moore.

Again a defensive error brought the goal.

Alan Ball, playing a dynamic role which demanded fantastic stamina and heart, sent over a corner from the right.

German centre-half, Willi Schulz, could not clear and the ball spun loose to Peters.

He bore down on Hans Tilkowski, a nervous keeper particularly in the first half, and shot fiercely.

PRESSURE

From then until the dying seconds, England piled up the goal chances.

"We made more than in all of the previous five World Cup games," admitted manager Alf Ramsey later.

But Hurst, Roger Hunt and Bobby Charlton all failed to grab the third goal which would sew up triumph.

A great victory roar was ready to detonate Wembley, ready to announce to the world that England were champs, when the Germans scored.

One of centre-half Jackie Charlton's normal but powerful defensive clearances was ruled a foul by referee Dienst thirty yards out... a harsh decision.

Lothar Emmerich's free kick punctured the English defensive wall. Haller appeared to handle and England's defenders claimed a foul.

IN THE MELEE WEBER GRABBED THE GOAL WHICH SENT WAVES OF DEPRESSION THROUGHOUT ENGLAND

Who could last out the longer? That was a big question.

Because each side had moments of ascendancy and the greasy top-surface caused by the rain showers did not help the players.

The refereeing controversy surrounding the Weber goal was nothing to that which followed.

There was panic in the German camp when the Russian linesman allowed Hurst's second goal – the score was now 3-2 for England, with twenty minutes of extra time to go.

The unrelenting pace was beginning to tell, the socks were

most German aggression.

The Germans were better marksmen. And they could never see themselves losing. What surprised the England side was the quiet role played by Franz Beckenbauer, the twenty-year-old "wonder boy" right-half who was expected to open up the play so dangerously.

Extra time proved England were a fitter team, that those long training sessions under Ramsey were worthwhile.

At the end when most of Wembley was yelling for Bobby Moore to kick the ball right out of the ground, Bobby started the fourth goal move.

From Moore to Stiles, on to Hurst, for the last goal with the last kick of a masterpiece thriller.

Let me spotlight the individual stars on this great occasion for English football.

Super-safety goalkeeper Gordon Banks, beaten only three times in the six matches – with England's record: Five games won, one drawn, eleven goals for, three goals against.

Right-back George Cohen, whose poise and speed subjugated West Germany's match-winner, Lothar Emmerich.

FLAWLESS

Left-back Ray Wilson whose one slip in this game should not obscure the flawless role he has played up to the final.

Right-half Nobby Stiles – undoubtedly one of the England mighty men. He could do no wrong yesterday. What inspiration flowed from his 5ft. 6in. frame.

Jackie Charlton, undoubtedly the centre-half stalwart of the tournament.

In the air, unbeatable, on the ground, able to take every forward pushed against him from Uruguay on July 11th to West Germany on July 30th.

Left-half Bobby Moore. World Cup success has always been traced to powerful captaincy.

He summed up the finest game of his career by saying: "At no stage of the game did I think England could lose."

Outside-right Alan Ball. If there are any in the football world who doubt his £105,000 category they should have seen his energy and class at Wembley.

coming down over the ankles, the faces were strained.

Just as Moore commanded the first half, he slipped into a tighter defensive role into the second, to cope with the wily Seeler.

STALWARTS

Alan Ball and Nobby Stiles were wonderful little stalwarts.

How they grafted, ball forever a dangerous roving raider; Stiles – well, Stiles was the pugnacious perfect destroyer of

Inside-right Geoff Hurst. Three goals in the World Cup final, leading English scorer of the tournament with four. He did his job with striking authority.

SUBDUED

Centre-forward Bobby Charlton: a quieter display in the final should not allow fans to forget his match-winning role earlier in the tournament.

Inside-left Roger Hunt: he worked hard throughout and had little luck. But the World Championship is won on a team effort. No finer team-man exists than Hunt.

Outside-left Martin Peters – growing in stature as the tournament progressed.

His second goal against Germany plus the vital one he made for Hurst against Argentina, justified his selection.

Do not let us forget on this great day the role of supremo Ramsey and his trainer lieutenants, Harold Shepherdson and Les Cocker.

ON THIS DAY

Economics minister George Brown ran into trouble with the unions over the Labour government's proposed prices and incomes bill... fashion designer Pierre Cardin launched a new "spaceman" look... Sir Stanley Matthews was in hospital in a "satisfactory condition" after a car crash... Architect John Webb, 75, complained to the local council in Southborough, Kent, when a girl wearing "just bra and pants" walked onto a tennis court overlooked by his office. "If I see a scantily clad girl on the courts again, I shall contact the council again."

World Cup Final	
England... (1) 4	West Germany... (1) 2 (aet.)
Peters 77	Haller 13
Hurst 19, 100, 120	Weber 89
	Att: 97,000

Gordon Banks saves surrounded by Jack Charlton, Ray Wilson, George Cohen and Martin Peters.

83

Scotland Conquers Europe

2-1! EUROPE BELONGS TO CELTIC

INTER DESTROYED AS SCOTS LIFT TOP CLUB PRIZE FOR BRITAIN

Celtic 2 Internazionale 1

Ken Jones

The banners waved and the hordes advanced. Celtic are Britain's first ever champions of Europe and they want the whole world to know about it.

Thousands of their followers have made the beautiful bowl of Lisbon's national stadium a madhouse of delight.

Billy McNeill, Celtic's captain, has stood high on the marble rostrum at the stadium's lip tonight, clutching the Cup that has eluded Britain's teams for so long.

He has stood like an Olympic torch-bearer, thrusting the silver trophy at the summer sky.

And Celtic's supporters have acclaimed him, cheering until they could cheer no more.

Inter Milan, famed, feared masters of football's professional arts, are back in their dressing rooms destroyed by Celtic's brilliant skill and unflagging effort.

Today the Italians were a side of shadows, desperately clinging to an early penalty goal lead and finally succumbing to the fierce endeavour of Celtic's football.

Certainly there can have rarely been a more one-sided final in the history of European competition.

It was played almost exclusively in Inter's half as they strove to contain the thrusts of green and white that stabbed at the heart of their defensive system. Inter began coolly and slowly in the afternoon heat, seeking to keep the game at their pace.

But there was deadly intent in two swift early attacks and in the third minute Celtic's goal might have fallen when a header from Mazzola struck goalkeeper Ronnie Simpson's legs.

In the sixth minute their goal did fall when Mazzola's through ball sent Cappellini hunting to the left of Celtic's Craig.

The tackle was badly timed, Cappellini tumbled to the lush green turf, and Mazzola strode up to score from the penalty.

It was the signal for Inter to fall back and summon all the defensive skills that had been drilled into them over the years in Italian football.

But there was carelessness in their play, and eagerness in Celtic's swift and urgent replies.

Bertie Auld struck a fierce shot against the face of the crossbar and Bobby Lennox and Jimmy Johnstone came close to equalising. A wonder save by Sarti from Tommy Gemmell's volley kept Inter's noses in front.

Then, in the second half, Celtic underlined the true quality of their teamwork and spirit.

Inter hung on, always desperately, often scrambling the ball away in a packed goalmouth.

And then, on the hour, came the goal that brought the first great chorus of their club's anthem from the Celtic supporters.

The ball went from Bobby Murdoch out to Craig on the right – and then back to be met by a thundering right foot shot from Tommy Gemmell who swept it high into the net past Sarti's right hand.

It was almost the same combination again as Celtic went on to get a glorious winner, five minutes from time.

Gemmell began it and when Murdoch's swift low ball penetrated Inter's penalty area, Steve Chalmers got the golden touch that gave Celtic the greatest of all club prizes.

Celtic captain, Billy McNeill.

European Cup Final

Celtic... (0) 2 Internazionale... (1) 1
Gemmell 60 Mazzola (pen) 6
Chalmers 85

Att: 60,000

Manchester Conquers Europe

FROM BRINK OF DISASTER... MATT'S NIGHT OF GLORY

THREE GOALS IN EXTRA TIME MAKE UNITED EURO CHAMPS

Manchester United 4 Benfica 1

Ken Jones

When the time has come to dim the emotion of this match, strong men will still remember it with tears in their eyes.

Manchester United have the European Cup. Their illustrious manager Matt Busby has finally conquered his Everest.

We shall remember it for what it meant to a great club, a great manager and to British football.

Above all we will remember it for the courage with which United hauled themselves out of a swamp of despair to break Benfica in the opening minutes of extra time.

With ninety minutes gone they were stretched like blue shadows on the green of Wembley's turf... sucking at the night air and desperately trying to slap life back into weary legs.

Busby hovered over them, hen-like – encouraging, anxious and fearing, perhaps, that the worst was to come.

The life had gone from his team late in the second half when Graca swept on to a Torres header to bring Benfica level after Bobby Charlton had nodded United into the lead in the fifty-second minute.

It suddenly seemed as though the tap had been turned off. United nearly fell as Eusebio, finding room among tired men, twice took Benfica close to triumph.

In the eighty-sixth minute he sprinted clear to bring a great save from Alex Stepney.

In the eighty-eighth minute he was clear again, arrowing his shot to Stepney's left only to find the goalkeeper brilliantly equal to the task.

Then it was extra time and the great cliff of red and white fans that rose behind United's goal waited anxiously to see which way it would go.

United needed a goal. And out of nothing they got it.

In the ninety-second minute Stepney, from the edge of his penalty area, drove the ball deep into the Benfica half. Brian Kidd helped it on and there was George Best, with only one man to beat and goalkeeper Henrique to come.

He squeezed the ball clear, drew Henrique from his line, swept wide of him and placed the ball into an empty net.

That goal acted on United like a massive dose of adrenalin.

Before eight more minutes had gone Benfica were broken beyond repair as first Kidd and then Charlton gave United an unassailable lead.

Suddenly it was over and Busby came from the touchline dignified but with his arms held wide.

He went to his players and then led them back to receive the trophy he has coveted for more than a decade.

Then he turned from them, refusing to take the merest flicker of their glory although the crowd echoed his name around the stadium.

It was not a great match. Indeed at times it was an ugly one.

Italian referee Lo Bello allowed it to get out of hand as players from both sides committed themselves to ruthless tackles in the first half.

Benfica's treatment of Best bordered on the disgraceful and full-back Cruz might have gone from the match long before the first half was finished.

In defeat Benfica do not retain the label of sportsmanship that the Portuguese acquired during the World Cup.

They showed their trite colours last night. It is difficult to admire anything they attempted.

United, too, were guilty of tackles that could not be excused by the emotion that surrounded the contest.

They made the better chances in the first half and there were times when Busby must have longed for the electric finishing of Denis Law.

It was the fifty-second minute before United got the goal that many believed would be enough to take them through to triumph.

David Sadler crossed from the left and Charlton glanced his header wide of Henrique's left hand and into the far corner.

Despite the skills of Best and Charlton it was their least recognised forward, John Aston, who commanded most of the admiration. He completely dominated full-back Adolfo.

Best had a mixed-up match, displaying great skill but robbing others of opportunities because of his greed on the ball.

But this was not a match from which to select individuals or to reflect on failure.

It was Manchester United's night. Matt Busby's night.

It was a match that the world was willing them to win. Perhaps it is enough that they won it.

Nobby Stiles and Bobby Charlton celebrate after the match. On the right is veteran Bill Foulkes.

ON THIS DAY

Senator Bobby Kennedy conceded he may have to drop out of the US presidential race... Charles de Gaulle was reportedly poised to quit as French President... The UK Government announced the housing crisis was due to end by 1973.

European Cup Final

Manchester United... (0) 4	Benfica... (0) 1
Charlton 52, 99	Graca 80
Best 92,	
Kidd 94	
After extra time	
	Att: 92,225

Another Cup Shock

SWINDON'S CUP GLORY

ARSENAL WERE ON THEIR KNEES AND DON ROGERS RUBBED IT IN

Arsenal 1 Swindon Town 3

Frank McGhee

Wembley has seen many great climaxes to many marvellous matches – the World Cup, internationals, FA Cup Finals.

But none of them, I swear, can do more than challenge the way the League Cup was won by humble, homespun Third Division Swindon. They bridged a canyon in class to crush First Division Arsenal in extra time.

The two Don Rogers goals in that half hour captured completely all the assets that send this player's value soaring.

The first reminded me with its cool control and pressure, of the great Hungarian Ferenc Puskas who once scored here, as Rogers was surrounded by men tensing themselves for lunging tackles.

Rogers gained possession in incredible confusion after the second of two corners in the fifteenth minute of extra time.

CASUAL GENIUS

He trapped the ball with a nonchalant flick, worked it briefly with the sole of his boot as he turned and waited for just the precise moment to hit it in with casual finality of genius.

Then, in the final seconds, with Arsenal dredging up the last

Victorious Swindon players.

they had left of stamina and spirit, the ball was pumped upfield by inside-right Roger Smart. And there, bursting irresistibly onto it, shoulders characteristically hunched, legs pumping, accelerating from the halfway line effortlessly away from any possible interception was Rogers.

He carried the ball into the penalty area, veered smoothly around the sprawling, lunging advance of Arsenal goalkeeper Bob Wilson, and drove it home.

This underlines a superiority that had already been emphasised earlier in extra time by a header from Smart that was tipped onto an upright by Wilson.

And yet when Arsenal had grabbed the equaliser four minutes from the end of normal time I wouldn't and couldn't have backed Swindon with someone else's money.

They should have been crushed psychologically by that eighty-sixth minute blow from Bobby Gould – a goal made all the more ironic by the contributory error of Swindon goalkeeper Peter Downsborough.

Until then, he had been a man revelling in acrobatics on a tightrope of tension.

Reading every situation correctly and responding with a series of marvellously agile saves under pressure as fierce as any Wembley has ever seen.

DESPAIRING BOOT

But in that eighty-sixth minute Downsborough mistimed a dash from his line to meet the thrust of Gould – sent on a streaking run by substitute George Graham – and found himself slithering outside his area.

He stuck out a despairing boot at the Arsenal inside-left's drive which floated in a high, lazy arc for Gould to challenge again – and head it into the still-empty net.

It is, however, equally true that Arsenal can blame not one error but four – within five seconds, more than they would normally make in a month – for the goal which cost them the lead in the thirty-fifth minute.

They had four separate distinct opportunities to win the ball before Smart scored.

Centre-half Ian Ure wasted the first, when inside-left

Peter Noble won a chase for a ball pumped down the left by Swindon skipper Stan Harland.

Goalkeeper Wilson was within touching, if not clutching, distance of it before it was hammered at goal by Noble and deflected to bounce equally between two challengers, Arsenal wing-half Peter Simpson and Smart.

Simpson, uncharacteristically, hesitated and conceded an important fraction of a second for Smart to drive on and win a ball that was deflected crazily enough to give Wilson another half chance of saving before Smart finally forced it over.

It came at the stage when it looked as though the inevitability of total Arsenal superiority, would take the edge off complete enjoyment for anyone except a sadist.

ONE MAGIC MOMENT

Until then, Swindon had had just one moment to savour.

In the tenth minute Rogers was given a chance to display his startling acceleration by a great through ball from Smart.

But he was foiled by a brilliantly timed rush from the line by the Arsenal keeper. Arsenal's control of the midfield through Radford and McLintock was enabling them to retain possession and attack constantly so that although the misses mounted – with Gould, Armstrong, Court and McLintock going close – it didn't seem to be more than a matter of time.

But after they had gone a goal down time suddenly became Arsenal's enemy and even more important luck deserted them also.

LITTLE LEFT TO OFFER

As events proved, the effort Arsenal put into getting their equaliser drained them physically and emotionally.

On their knees with expended effort, they had little left to offer. Swindon still had so much – notably the individual brilliance of Rogers – but it must be emphasised that he wasn't their only star.

Centre-half Frank Burrows and wing-half Harland were twin solid towers in their defence, while the way full-back John Trollope tried gamely to cope with the thrust of Radford, Arsenal's most dangerous forward, was a small masterpiece of diligence.

Celebrations outside the Town Hall.

League Cup Final

Arsenal... (0) 1	Swindon Town... (1) 3 (aet.)
Gould 86	Smart 35
	Rogers 105, 120

Att: 100,000

1969 Wednesday 11th June

No One Gave Them a Chance

HARVEY BRAVES RIP TO EUROPE GLORY

Ujpest Dozsa 2, Newcastle 3

Charlie Summerbell

Newcastle's sensational Fairs Cup victory here tonight was a magnificent boost for English football.

The Hungarian crowd generously applauded Bobby Moncur and his men as they carried the trophy on a lap of honour after their 6-2 aggregate win.

Newcastle were superb. Their chances of holding on to their 3-0 first-leg lead looked slight at half-time. The talented Hungarians, moving the ball with deadly accuracy, scored twice through Bene and Göröcs.

But in a fantastic burst in the opening minutes of the second half, Moncur, two-goal hero of the first tie, lifted Newcastle by slamming the ball home in the forty-eighth minute.

Two minutes and Preben Arentoft, Newcastle's Danish inside-forward, hit a second. And in the seventieth minute, teenager Alan Foggon, who substituted for Jim Scott, cracked in a great third.

It was an emotional moment for manager Joe Harvey, who skippered two Newcastle FA Cup winning sides at Wembley. It was also his fiftieth birthday.

Harvey told me: "I have not seen any Cup final or played in one that matched this game for excitement and fighting courage.

"It was remarkable by any standard to beat Ujpest on their own ground. I'm terribly proud of my boys and I know the whole city of Newcastle will be thrilled.

"We began as outsiders in the Fairs Cup and finished real champions."

Newcastle players arriving back at Newcastle airport; left to right Frank Clark, Ben Arentoft, Bob Moncur, Ollie Burton and Brian "Pop" Robson.

European Fairs Cup Final Second Leg

Ujpest Dozsa... (2) 2   Newcastle United... (0) 3

Ben 31   Moncur 48
Göröcs 44   Arentoft 50
                           Foggon 74

Newcastle win 6-3 on agg.

Att: 37,000

Brawling Takes Over From Football

IT'S THE BITTER END FOR LEEDS

JONES GIVES REVIE'S MEN A LEAD BUT WEBB LANDS EXTRA-TIME K.O.

Chelsea 2 Leeds United 1

Derek Wallis

For Leeds United manager Don Revie and Captain Billy Bremner along with Syd Owens the answer was a quick cuppa at Leeds station.

If there has ever been a more memorable and dramatic FA Cup final than the momentous replay at Old Trafford last night I am glad I am not old enough to have seen it.

The heart would not have survived. The lungs would have burst. The players would have collapsed through sheer exhaustion.

The pity, the tragedy of it all was that there had to be a loser.

A match of incredible tension and marvellous football, full of all the skills and endeavours of the modern professional, should have won prizes for both teams.

For Chelsea it was the familiar lap of honour, holding the Cup aloft in the unfamiliar surroundings of Old Trafford.

Whereas Leeds, their season in ruins after it had promised complete fulfilment, slumped dejected into the depressed area of the ground that was their dressing-room.

As Chelsea celebrated Leeds were left with nothing but the memory of a season which will show that in 1970 they won nothing – nothing, that is, except the admiration of those privileged to see two such great matches.

After getting within reach of a unique treble, Leeds first saw a repeat of their League Championship triumph crushed by Everton's challenge.

Their European Cup bid was ended in the semi-final by Celtic. Now the last hope – in the FA Cup – had gone.

It was inevitable that the result would not be settled in the normal ninety minutes last night.

Even when Leeds scored first, in the thirty-sixth minute,

brush marks to a masterpiece of a match.

The pace of the match, the quality of the football did not diminish even with extra time. Where these marvellous players found the reserves of energy is beyond me.

By extra time they should have been tiring, making errors, feeling the effects of a punishing season in the last match that offered the last chance.

Yet still they attacked each other with an almost maniacal relish, still playing wonderfully controlled football.

I know there were unpleasant fouls, that the physical contact often transgressed the bounds of legality.

That was largely the fault of referee Eric Jennings, an amazingly tolerant man whose control left much to be desired.

He reacted officially only once when he booked Chelsea's Ian Hutchinson for retaliating against Billy Bremner.

But who cares about the referee and the fouls when there was so much else to admire, so much drama on a night when the air crackled with tension, Leeds having established command in midfield, were the more impressive and penetrative in the first half.

More than once they held up their arms in disbelief as the ball refused to go where it would have counted.

Peter Lorimer was aghast at the injustice of it all when, running on to a pass by Johnny Giles, he beat David Webb and shot agonisingly on the wrong side of a post.

That touched off a spell of immense, awesome pressure by Leeds.

Eddie Gray, the scourge of Chelsea at Wembley, beat Ron Harris on the left and crossed a low ball into the middle, where Mick Jones forced Peter Bonetti to save at the foot of a post.

Then Eddie McCreadie cleared from Lorimer when Bonetti was stranded. A pass by Giles sent Bremner through and his short ball found Alan Clarke, who swivelled and shot – again the wrong side of the post.

Such intense pressure deserved a reward and Leeds won it with a goal that can best be described as one straight from the pages of football history.

Mick Jones, booed unmercifully by the crowd for a challenge that ended with Bonetti in pain and limping after

there was still a feeling of expectancy among Chelsea fans, still one of dread among Leeds supporters.

Chelsea left it late, almost too late for comfort. But they drew level – as they had done twice at Wembley – twelve minutes from time. And a minute before the interval of extra time they forced in the winner.

That is a capsuled comment. It does not tell of the magnificent football Leeds played for three quarters of the game.

It doesn't tell how Chelsea grew stronger as the match progressed, how they fought and challenged for every ball.

It doesn't tell of the wonderful goals that applied the final

Local support was strong in Chelsea.

team preoccupied with scoring a second and decisive goal.

Leeds failed fully to heed the warning. Chelsea equalised in the seventy-eighth minute.

Hutchinson started the move, Charlie Cooke produced an exquisite pass which left the Leeds defence stranded and helpless.

And Peter Osgood, who had moved stealthily into position, glided the ball in with a fine header.

Leeds returned to the attack. Gray skimmed the bar. A header by Jones from a cross by Lorimer also grazed the framework.

But Chelsea were back in the match and were at last Leeds's equals.

Still ninety minutes failed to settle it. Still they were at each other's throats. Still the destination of the Cup was uncertain.

After fourteen minutes of extra time Chelsea took the lead for the first time.

Hutchinson, the long-throw specialist, sent the ball curling wickedly into the middle where Jack Charlton's header only helped it farther.

As the ball dropped Chelsea surged in for the kill and appropriately, David Webb, who had been an unhappy man at Wembley, forced it over the line.

Chelsea skipper Ron Harris said: "We are always best when we come from behind – I reckon we deserved to win on the play in the second half."

Peter Osgood, describing his headed equaliser: "It made me feel terrific. It came from a lovely little curly lob from Charlie Cooke.

"They all look good in the back of the net, but this was something special."

Eddie McCreadie spared a thought for the losers: "Naturally we are delighted to win, but we have every sympathy for Leeds because they are a great side."

John Dempsey said: "I feel very sorry for Leeds. I hope they do all right next season."

prolonged treatment, answered the abuse in the only way he could – by scoring.

Clarke started the move in midfield, escaped one challenge, looked to have lost the ball and yet regained possession.

He beat off another Chelsea man, again reached a 50-50 ball first and sent Jones away.

Jones's path to goal was strewn with pitfalls.

Yet he hunched his broad shoulders, ran between John Dempsey and McCreadie and with John Hollins lurking near sent a devilish shot past Bonetti.

Somebody said the goal was a reminder of Ted Drake at his most devastating. It deserved the accolade.

The interval was only a temporary relief from pressure for Chelsea.

Leeds were playing with a power and precision designed to allow Chelsea little scope for one of their famous second-half comebacks.

But the warning was clear when David Harvey, stand-in goalkeeper for Gary Sprake, had to make his first serious save – a dive to stop Tommy Baldwin from scoring.

Chelsea began to make room for themselves, to attack a Leeds

David Webb scores the Chelsea winner.

FA Cup Final Replay

Chelsea… 2	Leeds United…1 (aet.)
Osgood 78	Jones 36
Webb 104	

Att: 62,078

South America Take It Away

BRAZIL SUNDAY PUNCH DOES IT

Brazil 4 Italy 1

Ken Jones

Brazil reclaimed the World Cup here today and with their third success made the Jules Rimet Trophy their own.

Here was the supreme triumph. The utter destruction of a vaunted and well-organised Italian defence.

A vindication of the romantic ideals that Brazil have pursued from their opening game in the competition.

The closing scenes were almost unbelievable as hordes of Brazilians, who had been waiting along the touchlines, swept over the victorious players, tearing the shirts from their backs and even pulling off them stockings and boots.

Italy, level at the sixty-sixth minute, were finally swept aside by a furious burst of attacking skills.

The Italians were reduced to a dispirited rabble by the time Carlos Alberto cracked in the fourth goal four minutes from time.

With the rain streaming down the weather was perhaps the final irony for those who believed that England should have been in the final with Brazil. Italy quickly threatened but Felix tipped for a corner Riva's shot on the run.

Rivelino was too high with a free kick after Jairzinho had

The referee has a quiet word with Italian, Giancarlo De Sisti as Pele watches.

DOMECQ
¡AGUANTAN!
ALFOMBRAS TAPETES
CASIMIRES
Perrott's
COMEX
Lo mejor en Pinturas
EXCELSIOR
INFORMA y FORMA OPINION
Pelikan
ARTICULOS PARA ESCOLARES

It's all over!

been pulled down.

Then Riva, let through by lax Brazil defence, shot when a pass to Boninsegna might have been more productive.

But it was first blood to Brazil in the nineteenth minute. And Pele was the scorer – all grace and skill as he rose above tall defenders to get in his header from the build-up by a Tostao throw-in and Rivelino centre.

All the attacking flair of Brazil and the generalship of Gerson could not obscure the flaws in defence and Italy were back in the game with an equaliser in the thirty-eighth minute.

Piazza had a clearance cut off and Brazil were in confusion as goalkeeperFelix committed himself to a challenge and Boninsegna clipped the ball into the vacant goal.

Burgnich was booked for a foul on Pele and Rivelino for a body check on Bertini who had gone in with a fearsome attempted tackle in the second instance. Brazil got the free kick and as the ball was crossed to him Pele had it in the net... but after the whistle had gone for half-time.

A spectacular goal restored Brazil's lead in the sixty-seventh minute, Gerson the general suddenly becoming the killer as he rounded off a move shared with Jairzinho. Three minutes later Italy were in deep trouble. Gerson resumed his role of creator to build the attack that put Jairzinho in for Brazil's third goal.

Pele headed Gerson's long forward pass down and across goal and Jairzinho flicked the ball through at the second attempt. Though Italy threw men forward in an attempt to save the game they had nothing to show for it.

And Brazil's triumph was complete four minutes from time.

Clodoaldo, Jairzinho and, finally, the master Pele, made a goal for skipper Carlos Alberto.

Pele's pass was perfectly measured into Carlos Alberto's stride and a wicked right-foot shot did the rest.

World Cup Final

Brazil... (1) 4	Italy... (1) 1
Pele	Boninsegna
Gerson	
Jairzinho	
Alberto	

Arsenal do the Double

GRAHAM AND GEORGE A DYNAMIC DOUBLE ACT

ARSENAL ROAR TO TRIUMPH WITH EXTRA-TIME GOALS

Liverpool 1 Arsenal 2

Frank McGhee

The Arsenal team prior to their FA Cup victory over Liverpool.

The half hour that saw Arsenal's dream of the double achieved must still seem barely believable – even to them.

It all happened in extra time at Wembley: thirty minutes of ordeal by exhaustion into which were crammed the emotions of a lifetime.

It was climaxed by the great goal which won it, slammed home from more than twenty yards by young Charlie George, who then flung himself on to his back where he lay quivering with joy.

But the drama has to start with the moment twenty minutes earlier when any exultation in the air was strictly reserved for Liverpool and their fans.

In the very first minute of extra time Liverpool had at last gone ahead in a game that had seemed certain to be settled by the first side to score.

To add to its drama, the goal was created by Peter Thompson, the man they sent on as a substitute to bring some ideas and initiative to the Liverpool attack.

From an inside-left position, the man who had replaced

Alun Evans midway through the second half, slid a ball out to centre-forward Steve Heighway on the left.

Heighway, until then anonymous, ineffective, submerged by the occasion, suddenly produced a flash of the dynamic, dramatic, running that has become his trademark.

He accelerated past full-back Pat Rice and cut in to slash a shot that went across diving keeper Bob Wilson and slammed inside the far post, bulging the side netting.

No side could have been deeper in despondency than Arsenal. Yet, ten minutes later they were level.

Centre-forward John Radford, standing with his back to goal, played a ball blindly over his head.

Eddie Kelly, who had also come on as a substitute in the second half for Peter Storey, seemed to have little chance of winning the ball.

Two of the great tacklers of the game, Emlyn Hughes and

Tommy Smith, were converging on him and Liverpool keeper Ray Clemence was also coming fast from his goal.

But Kelly managed to steer the ball to George Graham and the big, cool Scot accurately placed a shot that rolled over the line.

The odds still favoured a draw – until Charlie George received that John Radford pass in the sixth minute of the second half of extra time.

George summoned up all the startling, awesome power at his command to lash the ball in a blur past Clemence.

It was a marvellous moment. It contributed directly to an even more marvellous moment for one man – Arsenal skipper and Footballer of the Year, Frank McLintock.

This was the fifth time he has played in a Cup final at Wembley and the first time he has been on the winning side.

Yet all the emotions and congratulations cannot and must not be allowed to obscure the fact that this game was decided in an atmosphere of drama it did not deserve.

To put it bluntly, for its first ninety minutes this was the worst Cup final I have seen. And I have seen more than twenty.

It was ruined by two teams more obsessed by fear of failure than hunger for victory – until they became too tired to dredge up the energy for efficiency; so tired that they had to take chances and concede chances.

And that is NOT what this great game is supposed to be all about.

The first half was marked – or perhaps marred would be more appropriate – by the uncompromisingly ruthless tackling of Peter Storey.

A less tolerant referee than Norman Burtenshaw would not have allowed a couple of tackles on Heighway to go unnoticed.

And one hurtling foul on goalkeeper Clemence went right over the borderline which separates acceptable hardness from roughness.

Still, it must be conceded that Storey was the man who did most to ensure Arsenal's command of the midfield that they did not sufficiently exploit. For all the sparring and occasional breakaways, it was not until the thirty-ninth minute that the crowd rose and roared to the game's first great shot.

It was fired by Charlie George from fully thirty yards and it

Charlie George and his girlfriend.

skimmed the bar.

It aroused Arsenal to produce one of the few memorable moves, and moments, of the first half.

Two minutes from half-time, a cross from the right by Storey was met full tilt head-first by winger George Armstrong coming in from the left.

Clemence had to make a save compounded of instinct and ability to prevent the vital opening goal.

Immediately, Liverpool countered. A free kick by Tommy Smith was touched to left-back Alec Lindsay.

His shot was seen desperately late by keeper Bob Wilson who managed to touch it for a corner.

Liverpool were attacking only on the left. Arsenal were thrusting mainly down a middle inevitably sealed. It was a war of attrition: a stalemate. Very stale, mate.

Tommy Smith was not dominating for Liverpool. Neither were Simpson nor McLintock for Arsenal.

Chances arrived so rarely that it was remarkable to see George Graham involved in the two near misses in the seventy-eighth minute.

First a long throw from Radford was back-headed by him against the bar.

Then, from the resulting corner, Graham's header was blocked on the line by Lindsay.

I was beginning to think there would be no winner – and only one loser, the game itself – when extra time arrived to leave the fans with something to savour.

FA Cup Final

Liverpool... (0) 1   Arsenal... (0) 2 (aet.)
Heighway 91   Graham 101
                             George 111

Att: 100,000

Triumphant return to North London.

Yet Another Cup Upset

Hereford Utd 2 Newcastle Utd 1

Joe Cummings

Carpenter Ron Radford and sales rep Micky George carved with pride the name of Hereford United into the FA Cup history books. They did it with two golden goals that put the Southern League part timers into the Fourth Round and a home tie against West Ham next Wednesday afternoon.

And they will be remembered as the men who gave Hereford the record of being the first non-league club to beat a First Division team in the Cup since Yeovil k.o'd Sunderland twenty-two years ago.

Hereford earned their success with a fighting comeback after Newcastle had taken them apart in the first forty-five minutes of this Third Round replay.

Newcastle should have won easily but Malcolm Macdonald, Pat Howard and Terry Hibbitt missed easy chances in the first half. Hereford were transformed after half-time. With a cool, determined fury they attacked non-stop.

Dudley Tyler had a shot well saved by Willie McFaul and Colin Addison a header cleared off the line before Macdonald headed Newcastle ahead in the eighty-second minute.

Their lead lasted four minutes, Radford levelling with a thirty-five-yard shot.

Then came extra time and in the 103rd minute, George, a substitute for Roger Griffiths in the eightieth minute, right-footed the winner.

FA Cup Third Round Replay	
Hereford Utd... (0) 2	Newcastle Utd... (0) 1
Radford 85	Macdonald 82
George 103	
	Att: 14, 313

Ronnie Radford (left) and Ricky George who scored the goals.

Another Wembley Upset

GLORY, GLORY SUNDERLAND

HAIL THE WONDERFUL GIANT KILLERS

Leeds United 0 Sunderland 1

Ken Jones

Bob Stokoe's beaming, tearful face told it all at Wembley. The triumph was complete. Sunderland, from the Second Division and the very depths of improbability, had won the FA Cup.

The whistle had barely died on an astonishing upset when Sunderland's manager sprinted from the bench towards the goal his team had defended so heroically throughout the second half.

It was in that goal that Jim Montgomery had performed a football miracle with two super reflex saves inside two seconds from Cherry and then Lorimer just when it seemed that Leeds had broken through at last.

Montgomery, already engulfed by delight, was swept up into Stokoe's arms.

Leeds – every professional's choice as the best team in Britain, and probably Europe, too – had been beaten.

It was among the most remarkable of Wembley upsets – and the first Second Division success since West Bromwich Albion won the Cup and promotion in 1931.

Sunderland brilliantly supported their own confident prediction that killed off popular forecast and swept aside the theory that they were in danger of being outclassed.

Don Revie, suited, leads out Leeds, while Bob Stokoe in tracksuit looks like he means business.

Ian Porterfield.

But even allowing for Sunderland's ceaseless endeavour, the refusal to back down or to back off from illustrious opposition it must be said that Leeds threw it away.

Leeds had the better chances and they missed them. Clarke, unbelievably wasteful on the day, could and should have scored at least twice.

The crucial moment came in the thirty-first minute when Leeds had begun to hit something like normal form.

A Sunderland counter-attack brought them a corner and when Halom headed down, Porterfield drove in what was to be an historic winner.

Sunderland's midfield hustling, the speed of their counter-attacks and the unblemished play of centre-half Watson were outstanding features of the winners' game.

A rain-soaked surface made life difficult for defenders and a flurry of careless Leeds' passes gave Sunderland the chance to settle down quickly.

With the pitch slowing the ball, Leeds were forced to shorten their range but they threatened first with a Lorimer shot which went just wide.

Whenever Gray threatened Sunderland's vulnerable right-flank either Hughes or Kerr doubled back to help Malone.

Sunderland were in trouble when Clarke worked in from the right and three shots were beaten down before the ball was got away.

Mistakes were inevitable and when Leeds made another on the edge of their area, Horswill's instant shot was only just wide.

Sunderland were in no way overawed. They hustled as well as they were expected to in midfield and their willingness to go forward was refreshing.

With twenty-five minutes gone Sunderland had given away most free kicks but when Leeds' Clarke tackled Hughes from behind he was booked by referee Burns.

Leeds probed the far right side of Sunderland's goal hoping to send either Clarke or Jones in on crosses beyond turning defenders.

Leeds tossed away another chance in the thirtieth minute when Lorimer's cross from the right had Jones and Clarke in on the same ball. They immediately paid the penalty.

Sunderland broke to the other end and Harvey had to put Kerr's long forward ball away for a corner that turned out to be disastrous. Halom headed down Hughes's kick and Porterfield, with an astonishing amount of time, drove a dipping shot beyond Harvey's left shoulder.

It was all that Sunderland needed to sustain their enthusiasm and Leeds were left with an awful lot to do. They had no grip in the middle of the field and their whole game lacked customary assurance.

Sunderland played with so much confidence after their goal that Hughes set up an opening with a back heel to Kerr.

Watson's magnificent headwork blunted Jones and Clarke.

Gray, who was never given the time to weave a spell on the left-wing, might have been happier on a firmer surface.

Leeds barely got out of their own half in the ten minutes before half-time and Sunderland grew in stature all the time.

But when Leeds did get away, Watson produced a marvellous tackle to deny Clarke yet again.

By half-time Sunderland had achieved a lot of what they had attempted – crowding out Leeds in midfield and always able to threaten themselves.

Leeds just couldn't take their chances. The best had fallen to the usually deadly Clarke but it didn't look like his day.

Leeds started to put their game together at the start of the second half and were close to an equaliser when Montgomery, whose handling had always been uncertain, fumbled a long shot from Bremner.

Cherry had the ball in the net a minute later but Clarke had fouled Montgomery after Lorimer's cross and referee Burns gave a free kick.

Watson was superb, robbing Clarke with another perfect tackle when the Leeds striker was threatening along Sunderland's right.

It seemed to settle Sunderland and in one counter-attack Leeds had to beat out three shots before Guthrie drove into the side netting.

Referee Burns then denied Leeds what looked like a penalty when Bremner was pulled down by Watson. But Burns, to Leeds' disgust – waved play on.

Leeds pushed Bremner further forward, and almost immediately missed their best chance so far.

Cherry moved in beautifully on a slanted centre and when Montgomery made a superb diving save, Lorimer was left with an unguarded goal to aim at from three yards. But Lorimer could only screw his shot to the far side and Montgomery touched it out off the upright.

With Sunderland tiring, Clarke got through again, but his shot on the turn was deflected for a corner.

Gray was replaced by Yorath with ten minutes left and Sunderland had won another battle. Gray was the man Leeds had hoped would set Wembley on fire. He had done nothing.

Eight minutes from the end Hughes became the second man to be booked after a foul on Cherry.

Leeds produced a late flurry but it was a lost cause in front of goal. Cherry missed and they were in the market for a miracle. They waited in vain. It was Sunderland's Cup.

FA Cup Final	
Leeds United... (0) 0	Sunderland... (1) 1
	Porterfield 31
	Att: 100,000

The First Sunday Game in the Football League

SUNDAY STORM

SOCCER CHIEFS ATTACK "BLOODY-MINDED" MILLWALL

Millwall 1 Fulham 0

Harry Miller

League soccer on a Sunday came in yesterday to unqualified approval from the fans and ended with a bitter row.

Millwall, after attracting their biggest home gate of the season – 15,143 – against Fulham, then rejected Oxford United's request to play there in the Second Division next Sunday.

That, understandably, angered Oxford. Bob Kearsey, their chairman, heard of Millwall's refusal to switch from Saturday and blazed:

"I'm surprised and shocked. They are being bloody-minded. What Millwall are saying is that Sunday football is all right for them when they want it but not for other people.

"Surely, we all have to help each other during this emergency. I'm 100 per cent for Sunday football, particularly at a time like this.

"Millwall are the last club I would have expected to refuse our request. I'm bitterly disappointed.

"Millwall's decision will cost us between six and eight thousand spectators. After all, everyone else, including Millwall, has proved that a Sunday game draws the crowds."

Mick Purser, Millwall chairman, said: "Our gate against Fulham was well up on average. But we still don't think Sunday soccer should be a regular thing.

"We turned down Oxford because of the difficult travel involved for the players and supporters.

"It is also a fact that the players don't like Sunday football."

The little clubs, however – those from the Third and Fourth Divisions – now plan to get together for the right to play all their weekend games on a Sunday.

Walsall chairman Ken Wheldon said: "We want Sunday soccer permanently."

ON THIS DAY

Millwall's pioneering staging of league football kicking off on a Sunday morning came amid tortuous times for the country as a whole. Amid an oil crisis, industrial strife over Prime Minister Heath's pay restraint policy, and the three-day week, Britain was in a state of emergency, with power cuts a feature of daily life.

With floodlights banned, football clubs opted for Sunday kick-offs as a means to use electricity when demand was likely to be reduced compared to Saturdays. The short-lived experiment was a success: nine of the twelve clubs who played that Sunday recorded season-best attendances and every crowd was above average. In order to sidestep the archaic Sunday Observation Act which banned charging admission, clubs instead allowed "free" admission – but only if fans bought a match programme at the turnstiles.

Fans at the turnstiles waiting to get into their first Sunday game.

Football League Division Two

Millwall... (1) 1   Fulham... (0) 0
Clark

Att: 15,143

Total Football at its Finest

TWO-GOAL CRUYFF ROCKS ARGENTINA

Netherlands 4 Argentina 0

Holland showed the world last night it will need a formidable team to check their impressive march on football's greatest prize.

The Dutchmen produced football of breathtaking brilliance to destroy the fancied Argentineans. Now they are 6-4 World Cup favourites.

Master footballer Johan Cruyff was, tormentor-in-chief of the South Americans. He scored the first and last goals, made the third for Johnny Rep and proved too hot for Argentina to handle. Defender Ruud Krol roared up to slam Holland's other goal with a ferocious twenty-yarder after Argentina keeper Daniel Carnevali had failed to hold a corner.

With strikers Ruben Ayala and Hector Yazalde snuffed right out of it the Argentineans were never allowed to settle.

World Cup Second Round Group A	
Netherlands… (2) 4	Argentina… (0) 0
Cruyff 10, 90	
Krol 25	
Rep 73	
	Att: 56,548

POSTSCRIPT

This performance was arguably the greatest single display of the Dutch brand of Total Football. Pioneered at club level at Ajax, the strategy encompassed having skilful players throughout the team, set up in a fluid formation that enabled them to switch positions with ease.

The national side was managed in 1974 by Rinus Michels, one of the chief architects of the Total Football philosophy, and put into practice by a roster of superb players including Johan Neeskens, Ruud Krol, Johnny Rep and of course, the best of the lot – the legendary Johan Cruyff.

The South Coast's Finest Hour

LAMBS TO THE SLAUGHTER

FINAL FLING

Manchester United 0 Southampton 1

Ken Jones

Southampton not only shattered the odds, with a brave and truly remarkable victory at Wembley, they also finally ruined what once promised to be the most glorious season in Manchester United's history.

The dream of a League and Cup double had grown out of the momentum that United's eager youngsters built up through the dark months of winter.

They went to the final with only the Cup to play for but, it seemed with everything in their favour.

United had the style. They had the players – and Southampton are from the Second Division.

But by the time little Bobby Stokes sneaked through to strike the winner from McCalliog's pass nine minutes from time, United already looked a beaten team.

They suddenly looked ordinary, some of them like little boys lost on a day when they were expected to prove they have grown into men. United's rhythm had gone, broken up by tigerish Southampton tackling. With it had gone the confidence which has been central to their style.

Gordon Hill had gone too, the extrovert winger, who scored

twice against Derby in the semi-final, was on the bench and substitute McCreery was out there instead.

Hill had paid for his anonymity and his failure to overcome Rodrigues. Far from giving United the fillip of a different dimension, that change proved to be an adrenalin shot for the Saints.

They still had to win the Cup but a significant anxiety was clouding United's horizon.

Hill's departure also narrowed the threat of flank attacks and Channon had begun to find room in which to run.

It was a pass from McCalliog, so desperate to prove his former manager Tommy Docherty wrong, that did the damage.

There was a suspicion of offside when he split Buchan and Greenhoff with a forward pass. But Stokes was in and Stepney's left arm wasn't long enough to keep out the shot.

The problem then was to play out time, to avoid errors, as United thrust desperately forward.

A moment of inspiration, a flash of genuine initiative from Person, Coppell or McIlroy might still have saved the day for United's now silenced fans. But it was not to be and a wave of familiar Wembley emotion was unleashed at the end.

The massed ranks of Saints supporters, barely believing it was so true, danced on the terraces, a sea of the yellow their team wore on the day.

Their hero had to be big Jim Steele, a tower in defence.

And Paul Gilchrist, who wasn't sure he would be playing in midfield until late last week.

And Peter Osgood, who responded to a Cup final with conclusive proof that he has always been capable of reaching the topmost level of the game.

Osgood's career has been a curious mixture of enthralling skill and irritating inconsistency.

But on this day at Wembley, he had the skill to inject confidence into lesser team-mates and the athleticism to un-nerve United's defenders in the air.

The effect on goalkeeper Ian Turner was remarkable. He was so nervous in those opening minutes he dropped two shots, but on both occasions Clive Thomas had already blown.

Matching United's endeavour Southampton settled down to

Victorious!

feed Osgood and Channon with passes out of defence.

Osgood's headwork soon had Buchan and Greenhoff on edge and it was Greenhoff who conceded the first corner.

But the first moment of genuine anxiety was felt by Southampton when Hill survived an attempt to play him offside.

The winger galloped on to the edge of the box, but Turner had seen the threat and bulleted from his line to save one-handed.

Trouble threatened again for Southampton when Macari stole in behind their right-flank, then fired in a centre that caused panic.

At that stage, Southampton were living a little on their luck and relying heavily on the impressive Steele and his partner, Blyth.

It was then that Channon broke free, to stress that if the pass went in at the right time, United's defenders could be in trouble.

Channon sped towards goal, but Stepney was on his way and got a saving foot to the shot.

United got a breath of encouragement when Coppell, the best of their players, got away on the right. Pearson met the cross thunderously in front of the near post but the volley went wide.

Then came the moment when United could have taken it over. Hill's inswinging corner was touched on by Pearson and McIlroy, on the far side of goal, headed against the top of the upright.

Channon went dramatically close with a left footer, that Stepney was grateful to see fly wide, and Stokes gave a hint of things to come with a curler that dipped over.

His moment of glory came nine minutes from the end. For United it was all over. Their dream destroyed. Their self belief undermined by a team who had steadily gathered the conviction that they could win.

Man of the Match: Jim Steele (Southampton).

FA Cup Final

Manchester United... (0) 0 Southampton... (0) 1

Stokes 81

Att: 100,000

Liverpool Dominate Europe

WHAT A WAY TO GO!

SMITH AND KEEGAN CROWN IT FOR LIVERPOOL

Liverpool 3 Borussia Mönchengladbach 1

Frank McGhee

Two special men will remember and treasure this night, this game, this European Cup victory for the rest of their lives.

Tommy Smith and Kevin Keegan were not the only Liverpool heroes of an unforgettable night in Rome's Olympic stadium. The whole, lovely, lively lot of their players made it happen.

But for me it was the performances of this pair on the last time either will wear their famous red shirts – Smith is retiring and Keegan is leaving – which helps to make the occasion so memorable. Smith, one of football's originals, a tough guy with a heart, scored his first and only goal of the season at a crucial time for his team – restoring their lead when for the only spell in the game they looked like losing.

Keegan, quick, skilful and likeable, so tormented his personal "sentry", the great German defender Berti Vogts, that he won the penalty which made Liverpool's always deserved victory an absolute certainty.

But that is racing ahead of a story which demands to be told as it happened.

It wasn't only the Liverpool players who stole the show. Their fans, invading Rome in happy hordes, were as dominating on the terraces as their team were on the field.

Fears that the English champions might not be able to recover psychologically from their FA Cup final defeat by Manchester United last Saturday, were quickly squashed.

They went into this one in a mood of determination and dedication, and left the Germans with only memories of what might have been.

Those mostly involved Liverpool goalkeeper Ray Clemence, who produced saves of stunning quality when they were most needed.

He was lucky only once, early in the first half when a shot from Rainer Bonhof struck a post.

A goal then – in the twenty-second minute – would have been savage injustice for Liverpool.

They set out and succeeded in taking over the game. The first goal came in the twenty-eighth minute when Steve Heighway rolled a sweet ball from Ian Callaghan into the stride of Terry McDermott.

Goalkeeper Wolfgang Kneib was criticised by some for not coming out more quickly but McDermott struck his shot so incisively that there was never a chance of saving it.

It was the desperation of their situation which prompted Borussia to push men forward at the start of the second half.

It brought an immediate reward when their little Danish striker Allan Simonsen equalised in the fifty-first minute.

But it still took a terrible error by a Liverpool player, midfield man Jimmy Case, to make it possible. He played a careless ball back towards his own goal and Simonsen nipped in.

This was when Clemence took over. He had to make a great save from Stielike and must have been grateful when Simonsen was only just wide with a header.

Liverpool's rhythm was interrupted at this stage. They were stuttering and spluttering and it was all against the run of play when they went in front again.

Klinkhammer conceded a corner and from Heighway's cross Smith got in a glorious header to make it 2-1.

I was just beginning to think that Borussia were accepting their fate when they made their final bid for victory.

Once again, Clemence had to make a marvellous save on the edge of his penalty area as Heynckes and Simonsen challenged him for a cross from Stielike.

But Liverpool made absolutely certain of victory in the eighty-third minute when the exasperated Vogts, frustrated by trying to mark a man who on the night was too good for him,

hauled Keegan down.

It was a blatant foul in the penalty area and Phil Neal scored from the spot with his customary coolness.

Ref Robert Wurtz could easily have blown his whistle to signal the finish right then. Borussia were finished and looked it.

Bob Paisley and Kevin Callaghan, true love!

European Cup Final

Liverpool... (1) 3 Borussia Mönchengladbach... (0) 1

McDermott 28   Simonsen 51
Smith 65
Neal (pen) 83

Att: 57,000

Scotland's Almost Finest Hour

SCOTS' FIGHTING EXIT

THREE GOALS NOT ENOUGH TO HALT DUTCH

Scotland 3 Netherlands 2

Frank McGhee

Scotland's hopes of a World Cup miracle flickered and then died against Holland here last night.

It looked as if they would do the impossible when two second-half goals by Archie Gemmill – one a penalty – put Scotland 3-1 up.

But then the Dutch came back to score through Johnny Rep to make the three-goal margin the Scots needed as elusive as ever.

Scotland swept down on the Dutch in the opening minutes but their appalling luck continued.

Graeme Souness made a super cross and Bruce Rioch jumped to head the ball. He got it expertly and then sadly it bounced back off the crossbar with Jongbloed beaten.

Nevertheless, this was the kind of early inspiration the determined Scots dearly needed. The Dutch, playing a 4-3-3 formation, were upset by an injury to Neeskens, who appeared to injure himself as he tried to tackle Archie Gemmill. Neeskens was carried off and replaced by Jan Boskamp.

Tom Forsyth had the ball in the net but the whistle had clearly gone for offside before he did so. Kenny Dalglish also

beat the goalkeeper with a perfect chip, but the Austrian referee knocked this off for a foul by Joe Jordan a few seconds earlier.

Scotland in these vital early minutes certainly looked better than they had done against Peru and Iran. They hustled and harried the Dutch, and pressed them into making chancy passbacks.

HUSTLING

When Jordan was tumbled down by Suurbier after eighteen minutes, Argentineans whistled angrily from the terracing when a penalty claim was rejected.

Their first real success, in fact, was a corner conceded by Willie Donachie after twenty-one minutes. When the ball came over Hartford headed it out and Forsyth had to jump to head out the next.

Souness tried vigorously to make Scotland tick. A long pass from him to Bruce Rioch ended with the Dutch happily conceding a free kick on the edge of the box. Souness took it, but the ball was kicked away as Dalglish tried to head it in.

Astonishingly, Scotland had a tremendous gang of supporters in the vast Mendoza stadium. They cheered every move by the Scots in their last-ditch effort to restore credibility to Scottish Soccer.

BLUNDER

The first genuine shot at the Scottish goal was after twenty-five minutes. Van Der Kerkof hit the ball low – but wide. Rough was hurt when he leapt to hold a header and Rep lunged against him and rammed him against a goalpost.

After thirty-four minutes the bottom was knocked right out of the Scottish effort.

Holland were gifted a penalty and Rensenbrink scored expertly. It was a blunder by Stuart Kennedy, who lost the ball to Rep and then tried to recover and tackle the Dutch player

along with Rough. The referee said it was a penalty, but it looked a poor one to me.

In the row which followed the penalty the referee showed the yellow card to Gemmill, who had thrown the ball angrily in his direction.

Dalglish made a good break on the right and crossed into the danger area. Jordan won his jump with keeper Jongbloed, but the ball went narrowly wide.

Rensenbrink had every reason to be specially pleased with himself. It was flashed up on the giant scoreboard that his goal was the 1,000th goal scored in the World Cup.

A minute from half-time Scotland equalised. Souness made a perfect cross, Jordan nodded the ball down and Dalglish whacked the ball into goal with his right foot.

It was a magic moment for Scots in the 50,000 crowd. Just after this Holland made another substitution when Risbergen limped off and Wildschut came on.

The impact Souness continued to have on the game was enormous. He was in so swiftly and venomously on to a cross from the right by Dalglish in the forty-seventh minute after a short corner that the only answer the Dutch had was a foul.

RAMPANT

Souness was cut down with blatant illegality by Dutch sweeper Rudi Krol and from the inevitable penalty Gemmill smashed right-footed the goal that made it 2-1 for Scotland.

Now the Scots really were rampant. They were at last playing the way they had promised they would. Too late, of course, but at least and at last they were giving the World Cup something to remember of them.

POSTSCRIPT

Despite producing arguably the nation's greatest ever performance, Scotland narrowly missed out qualification for the next phase. The team had travelled to Argentina with great fanfare – manager Ally McLeod famously claimed his side would win the World Cup. Defeat to Peru and an embarrassing draw with Iran put those ambitions in stark perspective, but the win over the mighty Dutch at least restored Scots' pride.

Archie Gemmill scores Scotland's third goal.

World Cup Group 4

Scotland… (1) 3
Dalglish 44
Gemmill 47 (pen), 68

Netherlands… (1) 2
Rensenbrink (pen) 34
Rep 71

Att: 35,130

125

1978 Wednesday 29th November

The First Black Player to Play for England

THIS NEW BOY'S REAL COOL, MAN!

England 1 Czechoslovakia 0

It wasn't long before he was showing Wembley last night what Forest fans already know – that he is a very cool customer. The occasion did not ruffle him, nor did world-class Czech winger Zdenek Nehoda. It was not an easy debut for Viv, but he coped in a way that suggests this could be the first of many caps.

He began the move that led to England's winner, and drew this praise from manager Ron Greenwood: "With such speed of recovery he was saving and diverting many dangerous situations. He was delightful, and to be involved in the goal was a bonus."

But Viv's mother, Mrs. Myrtle Anderson, was not at the game. Instead – out of a sense of duty – she went to work as usual at Highbury Hospital, Nottingham.

Viv didn't lack family support, though. His father Audley, a security officer, and his eighteen-year-old brother Donald were there to cheer him on.

International	
England... (0) 1	Czechoslovakia... (0) 0
Coppell 68	
	Att: 92,000

Four years later at the World Cup in Spain, Viv's still the only black player in the "team" photo.

FA Cup Final Classic

GLORY BE, ARSENAL!

OH, THE ECSTASY AND THE AGONY

Arsenal 3 Manchester United 2

Ken Jones

Wembley has staged no greater drama than that which erupted in the dying moments of what became a momentous Cup final.

With just four minutes left, Arsenal looked safe, leading 2-0, playing out the time that divided them from a triumphant circuit of the great stadium.

It was then that United suddenly came bursting out of nowhere, dredging up one last surge of energy and spirit to astonish us with a unique Wembley comeback.

Arsenal had just brought off the flagging Price and replaced him with Walford.

Almost immediately, United struck, the giant McQueen taking Jordan's low cross to drive it past Jennings.

They were playing into the faces of their own fans, banked high on the terraces behind Arsenal's goal.

And that bank came fully alive again as though sensing that there was more drama to come.

United, celebrating that goal with exhorting fists, lanced forward again.

Coppell sent McIlroy through on the left-flank of Arsenal's defence and the slim Irishman, peeling square across field, stroked an equaliser into the far corner.

Salvation for United – or so it seemed – as their manager, Dave Sexton, and his compatriots on the touchline bench leapt in jubilation.

But the joy was short-lived, as Liam Brady applied his genius once more to Arsenal's cause.

From deep in the right-hand corner of United's half and just when we were tolling off the seconds to extra time, Brady sent an immaculate pass to Rix, who crossed perfectly from the left for Sunderland to convert triumphantly from wide of the far post.

That was it, and as Arsenal gave themselves up to an explosion of joy, the United players slumped to the turf in tearful despair.

Three goals in three minutes. Heart-stopping stuff that erased the memory of what had been until then a largely dull and often shoddy final.

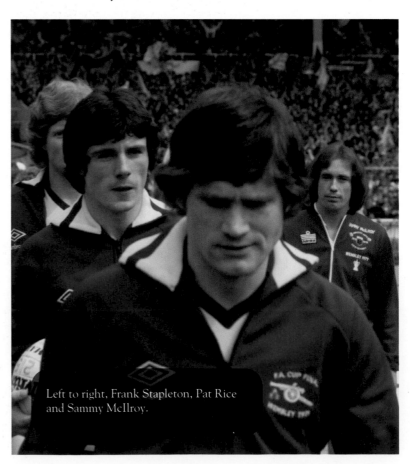

Left to right, Frank Stapleton, Pat Rice and Sammy McIlroy.

Alan Sunderland.

Rising above all that was Brady, the Irishman who is now fully established as one of the great natural talents in the game.

A year ago, Brady limped forlornly out of the final against Ipswich, a half-fit failure promising to do better the next time.

That promise was emphatically fulfilled as he produced two flashes of genuine class to make two goals that by half-time had seemed to have won the Cup for Arsenal.

United's dilemma all week had been to try and contain Brady within the overall pattern of their play or to detail one man to keep him quiet.

They settled for giving the responsibility to Macari, but it was neither one thing nor the other.

Brady began quietly though determined to get the true feel of pitch soft enough to send the most balanced players slithering embarrassingly onto their backsides.

Then in the twelfth minute Brady produced a run that was to tear United apart.

Three men tried to smother him, but the ball stayed close to that educated left foot.

It went then to Stapleton, then to Price, who, keeping his head, drove a low pass amidst the flailing feet in United's penalty area.

Sunderland and Talbot piled in. Sunderland got the first touch but looked like Talbot sent the ball into the roof of Bailey's net.

It was Brady's significant contribution, but now he began to press that he was the most important figure in the match.

Nevertheless, United had their moments and, in fact the better chances in the first half.

Thomas, close in, struck a first-timer from McIlroy's pass that flew straight at Jennings.

Jordan, who looked at times as though he was capable of leaping right out of the stadium, raked the crossbar with a header.

And then after Rice, Arsenal s captain, had been booked for obstructing McIlroy, United produced their most effective combined effort of the first half.

Jordan and Thomas were involved and Greenhoff was only inches away from what would have been a spectacular goal as,

on the turn, he drove just over the top.

Then it was Macari's turn with a header that once again found Jennings perfectly placed to deal with the threat.

That combination of expert positioning and good fortune was to prove decisive on the day.

Even more so was the goal that came in the forty-fourth minute as Brady flowered once more.

It was almost in slow motion as he looked up, measured the distance and found Stapleton, who, criminally unmarked on the far post, headed an easy goal.

United for much of the second half looked to have given themselves up to defeat and Arsenal, inspired by Talbot's relentless energy, seemed to have the game well in hand.

For a while we were treated by Brady to examples of his talent. The dribble, the pass slotted immaculately between defenders.

Arsenal might have gone further in front when Stapleton sent in a header that Bailey just got to with his knees.

Jennings saved Macari's header, pushing it over the bar brilliantly one-handed.

Talbot made an important tackle on McIlroy, Macari hooked over and Jennings, that combination of skill and luck working for him again, was right in line when Coppell volleyed fiercely.

Even so, there was no hint of the drama to come and Nicholl only just managed to foil Sunderland when the Arsenal forward dived at a Rice centre.

Then suddenly it all happened – almost a bizarre happening.

Whenever Cup finals are talked about, the finish to this one won't be forgotten.

FA Cup Final

Arsenal... (2) 3	Manchester United... (0) 2
Talbot 12	McQueen 86
Stapleton 44	McIlroy 88
Sunderland 89	

Att: 100,000

Frank Stapleton jumps for the ball ahead of Martin
Buchan, watched by Gordon McQueen.

European Underdogs

TWO TIMER

CLOUGH'S HEROES HANG ON AFTER ROBBO STRIKES

Nottingham Forest 1 Hamburg 0

Frank McGhee

Brian Clough's Nottingham Forest remain Champions of Europe.

They kept that great gleaming trophy in their cabinet with a performance here last night that captured everything that is best in the British game.

This European Cup final contained some truly magnificent goalkeeping.

Peter Shilton will never make finer saves than a couple he produced in this match.

It had a goal worthy of winning any trophy from John Robertson, that chubby, tubby, unlikely-looking winger.

It had stubborn defensive resistance from every angle on view, and from two in particular, Kenny Burns and Larry Lloyd.

Between them they managed to make even Kevin Keegan look ordinary long before the end.

There was tireless, selfless running from Garry Birtles upfront. He gave everything and then found some more.

But if I had to single out one individual star it would have to be the Irish midfield man Martin O'Neill, who must have stepped on every blade of grass on the pitch. He had a magnificent match.

Forest had their warnings that it might be rough when Hamburg defender Manny Kaltz went right through Robertson to win the ball seconds after the start.

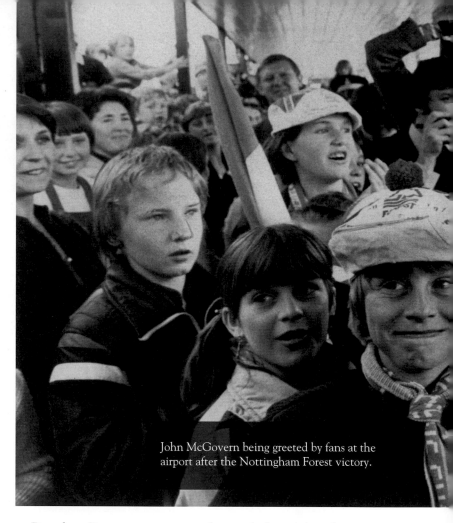

John McGovern being greeted by fans at the airport after the Nottingham Forest victory.

But then Burns was not exactly gentle in cutting down striker Jurgen Milewski within the next half minute.

The stage was already set for a tough tussle with Burns dedicating himself to subduing Keegan.

It was Lloyd however, who cut down Keegan in the eighth minute and gave the Germans their first clear shot at goal.

Shilton had to be really sharp to beat away a free kick touched by Milewski to Felix Magath.

Forest were uncharacteristically content to sit back and soak up all the pressure. For too much of the early play they left Birtles alone up front.

It was an invitation to the Germans to attack and no one accepted the invitation more eagerly than Kaltz.

But Hamburg's aggressive attitude rendered them wide open to the sort of counter-attack Forest mounted in the seventeenth minute. Viv Anderson made a cute interception deep in his own half and after a long, strong run, sent Birtles in for the first authentic shot of the match.

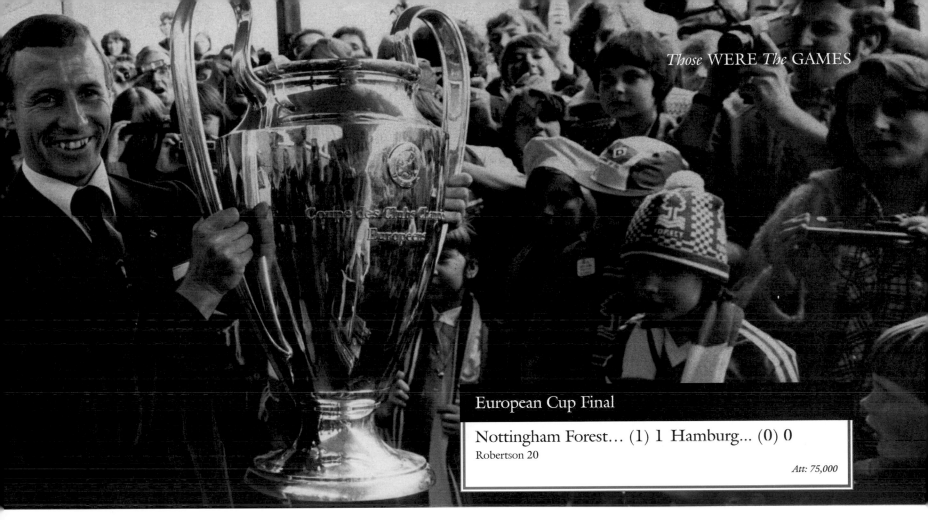

European Cup Final

Nottingham Forest... (1) 1 Hamburg... (0) 0
Robertson 20

Att: 75,000

It was followed three minutes later by the game's first magic moment – a goal from Robertson, with the considerable co-operation of Birtles.

After a wriggling run down the left which took him clear of Kaltz, Robertson snapped up a return pass from Birtles.

From the edge of the penalty area, he hit a shot which went in off a post.

Forest had a fright thirty seconds later, when Hamburg were denied an equaliser from Willi Reimann as Keegan was stranded offside.

In a frantic burst of German activity, Burns was booked for a foul on Keegan.

Even neutrals had to agree that Hamburg were worth an equaliser in the thirty-third minute when Shilton made the save of a lifetime.

Kaltz pumped the ball forward, and Keegan chested it down, right into the stride-path of Milewski.

The Forest keeper coped magnificently, beating away a powerful shot for a corner.

Hamburg started the second half with a gamble, bringing on their injured striker Horst Hrubesch and removing midfield man Helgar Hieronymus.

The Germans continued to do most of the forcing but, as the minutes dribbled away, they began to lack conviction. Even Keegan was forced deeper and deeper in his attempt to create space for himself.

Then, in the sixty-sixth minute, Forest had the narrowest escape of the whole evening when striker Magath smashed a shot against the outside of an upright, with Shilton helpless.

Forest made a substitution a minute later, calling off teenager Gary Mills and reinforcing the midfield with John O'Hare.

Hamburg defender Peter Nogly got the yellow card for a cruel foul on O'Neill – and then forced a tremendous save from Shilton with a thirty-yard drive.

In the end, that one goal by Robertson was enough to keep the European Cup in England for the fourth successive year.

EA Cup Final – The Classic Replay

FAIRY TALE FINISH FOR SPURS

ANGRY VILLA BOUNCES BACK

Tottenham 3 Manchester City 2

Frank McGhee

You could not write as fiction and have it accepted the story of the match Ricky Villa played. Or the goal he scored to win the 100th FA Cup final for Tottenham in last night's Wembley replay.

The big Argentine international finished the first meeting on Saturday in a mood of rage, despair and humiliation at being substituted. Last night he scored twice – and his Cup-winner was one of the greatest goals Wembley has ever seen.

He took the ball on a long, strong solo run past two Manchester City defenders before smacking it in with authority, style and power in the seventy-seventh minute.

It provided a fitting climax to what will rank as one of the best Cup Finals ever seen.

Spurs outnumbered City at the start, but only nearly, in the larger number of fans, who had to pay far smaller sums to get to the game.

They outnumbered City with men on the field, who, from the start, were prepared to battle for the ball – and it is as well for them that they were in that sort of mood.

After Ossie Ardiles had survived a crunching tackle by Gerry

Gow almost before the echoes of the first whistle had died away, City had one chance for Steve Mackenzie beaten away by keeper Milija Aleksic.

Then another came and went when the big, bearded Ricky Villa got in a penalty-area tackle which robbed Kevin Reeves.

Spurs went ahead in the eighth minute when Ardiles made one of those lovely, intricate little runs that have become his special trademark.

He sent Steve Archibald in for a shot so venomous that even a goalkeeper as good as Joe Corrigan in his most combative mood could only parry.

It was Corrigan's misfortune that, waiting to pounce on that rebound, was the one Spurs player with a special, personal stake in this game – the Villa who danced his delight and enjoyed his congratulations after he had scored.

It was difficult to realise that a magnificent, memorable match was only eleven minutes old when City got their equaliser.

The goal came from a spectacular twenty-yard shot by Mackenzie that ranks in impact and importance with any I have seen on this great ground.

It started with a free kick headed back across the penalty area by Tommy Hutchison, half cleared by gutsy Graham Roberts, but then struck with such sudden, stunning power by Mackenzie that no goalkeeper in this world could have stopped it. The match went on like that – so full of incident that it became difficult to cram them all into one story.

But the longer it went on and the more those incidents mounted, the more obvious it seemed that there was a sharper point, a deadlier purpose, to Tottenham's attacks.

Corrigan had to be as good as he is to beat away for corners two shots from Villa.

He was very lucky once when a free kick shot by Glenn Hoddle scraped the paint from the wrong side of an upright.

The men who were doing so much for Tottenham were their Argentine pair, Ardiles and Villa, so utterly unlike in physical appearance but twins in their regard for the game.

Spurs, if anything, intensified their pressure at the start of the second half, which produced the controversial moment when City went in front.

FA Cup Final Replay

Tottenham... (1) 3	Manchester City... (1) 2
Villa 8 min, 77 min	Mackenzie 11 min
Crooks 70 min	Reeves (pen) 50 min
	Att: 92,000

There really should be no controversy. Spurs defender Paul Miller quite clearly shoved City striker David Bennett off the ball illegally inside the area in the fiftieth minute.

Reeves had no trouble at all in scoring from a properly awarded penalty. City right-back Ray Ransom was booked for a foul on Ardiles. Spurs forward Tony Galvin was similarly punished for a slash at Hutchison.

Gow went into the book for another hack at Ardiles. Archibald was booked for dissent.

Four cautions in the space of six minutes must create some sort of record.

Spurs fought desperately hard for an equaliser – and got it in the seventieth minute through Garth Crooks.

He toe-poked the ball in following a corner kick.

East Anglia Conquer Europe

IPSWICH NIGHT OF FRIGHT

BUT THEY RIDE OUT STORM AND TRIUMPH

Ipswich 2 AZ Alkmaar 4

Jack Steggles

Ipswich put themselves on the torture rack here in the Olympic stadium last night as they were crowned UEFA Cup kings.

They made themselves – and the 7,000 travelling fans – suffer agonies before marching up proudly to collect the trophy.

It's a rich and fitting reward after a memorable season and Ipswich fully deserve the rapturous welcome home they will get today.

But for much of this second leg of a final that can only be described as bizarre, they seemed to have a death wish.

We had been assured that the team with a reputation for wobbling when they had big leads in Europe would make no such mistake this time.

But it never worked out like that and some uncharacteristic defensive slips presented Alkmaar with gifts no team has a right to expect at this level. Alkmaar – trailing by three goals from the first leg – had to throw everything they had at Ipswich.

Ipswich had been warned to expect it. But they still did not seem prepared, and their faithful fans were in a sweat of anxiety on a hot steamy night with temperatures up in the 70s.

Edge of your seat football.

Medisport

The Ipswich players were in a sweat as well, as Alkmaar put them under fearful pressure in a bid to save the game.

Their manager George Kessler had demanded they run until they dropped. And he could not have got more out of them.

Their all-out attacking left them vulnerable at the back – and Ipswich took advantage to grab the goals that gave them the trophy.

Celebrations begin!

They could not have asked for a better start, with Dutch international Frans Thijssen celebrating his return home by smashing them into the lead after just four minutes.

Thijssen is in dispute with Ipswich and threatens to take his immense talents elsewhere.

If he does decide to leave he could not have given Ipswich a better going-away present.

That goal left Alkmaar needing five to win and should have taken all the pressure off Ipswich.

But it didn't. They allowed Alkmaar to equalise three minutes later, Kurt Welzei heading through a centre from Johnny Metgod after Paul Cooper came for a long through ball, failed to get it and was left stranded.

Alkmaar went ahead on the night after twenty-four minutes, when Metgod was allowed to rise unchallenged at the far post to head through a centre from Jan Peters.

Ipswich, facing only two men at the back, looked like scoring every time they went forward.

And John Wark equalised for them with an overhead kick in the thirty-first minute.

It was his fourteenth goal in Europe, equalling the record set by Jose Altafini, of AC Milan, in 1963.

More defensive uncertainty allowed Pier Tol to restore Alkmaar's lead six minutes before half-time.

And the game was really thrown wide open when Jos Jonker scored Alkmaar's fourth with a blazing thirty-yard free kick after seventy-two minutes.

Alkmaar smelt blood now and moved menacingly in for the kill. But Ipswich dug deep into their reserves of courage to hold out and take the trophy.

Manager Bobby Robson acknowledged the score they had had when he said: "We were on a knife edge.

"We needed the three goals we got in the first leg.

"They threw men at us from all over the place but they did not have any other option.

"I'm delighted for everyone at the club and this goes a long way to make up for all the earlier disappointments we have suffered."

UEFA Cup Final

Ipswich... 2	AZ Alkmaar... 4
Thijssen	Weld
Wark	Metgod
	Tol
	Jonker

HT: 3-2 Ipswich win 5-4 on aggregate

Att: 28,500

The First Football League Game Played on Plastic Pitch

CARPET BAGGERS!

LUTON STEAL AWAY WITH THE POINTS

QPR 1 Luton 2

Harry Miller

The space-age party which was meant to launch Rangers on a magic carpet road towards the First Division ended with Luton doing the celebrating.

Rangers walked from the pitch of the future deep in the realisation that old-fashion mistakes will be punished on any surface.

Talented Gerry Francis made one error six minutes from time – and Ricky Hill scored to take the shine off a memorable evening for Rangers chairman Jim Gregory and his enterprising board.

What that should not do is to disguise the fact that Rangers appear to have a winner with their £300,000 artificial pitch, the first for professional use in Europe.

It's a surface man-made for skill.

No longer will teams come to Shepherd's Bush and complain about a surface which was once among the worst in the League.

Whether bigger, more glamorous clubs will follow the ambitious lead of Rangers only time will tell.

It is an experiment the Football Association particularly are watching with a certain scepticism.

It should be said that the real test will come as the harsh winter months begin to bite.

Luton themselves could not make a better investment than this type of synthetic surface. They are certainly a skilful side.

They have maximum points from their first two matches and manager David Pleat said: "We were happy with the pitch. It played faster than we thought.

"As the season goes on, a lot of people will be in trouble here because Rangers have got skilful players."

Luton trailed after thirty-four minutes. Bob Hazell crossed and Andy King headed in at the far post.

Luton steadied themselves in the second half, played the ball more to the feet, and deservedly equalised in the seventieth minute.

Ricky Hill, my man-of-the match, provided the pass for left-back Mark Aizlewood to lob over John Burridge.

Luton's winner, after eighty-four minutes, came when Francis lost the ball to Steve White, and Hill scored with a stunning drive.

Football League Second Division

QPR... 1 (1)	Luton... (0) 2
King	Aizlewood
	Hill
	Att: 18,703

POSTSCRIPT

QPR's plastic pitch experiment lasted until 1983, when the FA enforced a ban. Other clubs had also laid artificial turf, including Oldham Athletic and Luton.

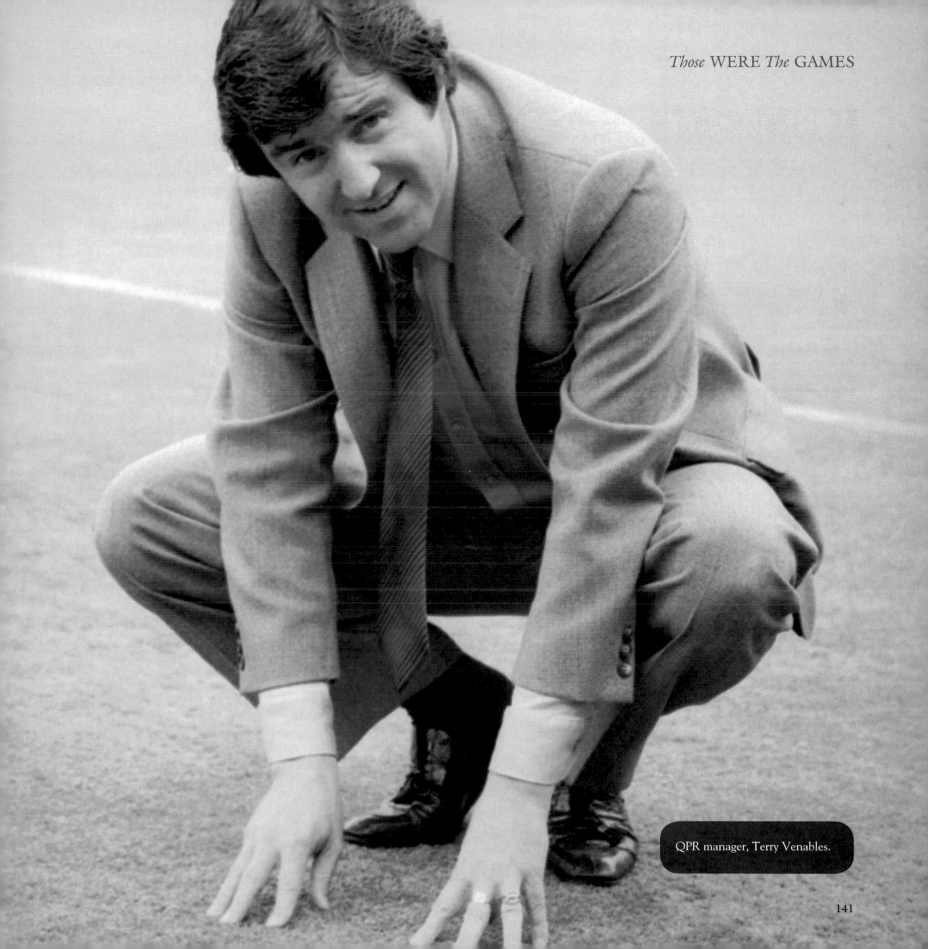

QPR manager, Terry Venables.

Revenge for Italy – an Absolute Cracker!

ROSSI DOES THE TRICK

ITALY'S BLACK SHEEP BLASTS OUT BRAZIL

Italy 3 Brazil 2

Paolo Rossi scored a glorious hat-trick to send favourites Brazil tumbling out of the World Cup yesterday.

Rossi, the golden boy of Italian football until he was banned for his part in a match-fixing scandal, ended South American interest in the tournament and plunged soccer-mad Brazil into mourning.

But Rossi wasn't the only hero in a stunning display by Italy. Veteran goalkeeper Dino Zoff marked his 104th international with a string of brave saves, particularly in the face of a desperate late onslaught by Brazil.

So the dazzling Brazilians leave a competition they have graced, paying dearly for some poor defensive play for which even their skills could not compensate for in a packed Sarria stadium.

Italy, needing a victory to earn a semi-final meeting with Poland, made a dream start by going ahead in the fifth minute.

Bruno Conti's crossfield pass set Antonio Cabrini free on the left and his cross to the far post found Rossi unmarked to head past keeper Valdir Peres.

Serginho missed a sitter before skipper Socrates levelled for the odds-on favourites seven minutes later. A swift exchange of passes with Zico sent him clear of the defence and he squeezed a low shot between Zoff and the near post.

A minute later Israeli referee Abraham Klein booked Claudio Gentile for a crude lunge at Zico – a costly foul for the Italian defender who now misses the semi-final after two bookings.

Brazil then took control, but again were caught out in the twenty-fifth minute. Cerezo's loose midfield pass was intercepted by Rossi, who shot past Peres from the edge of the box.

Italy had to re-organise the centre of their defence when Fulvio Collovati was injured in the thirty-third minute and replaced by Giuseppe Bergomi of Inter Milan.

Falcao had a shot deflected wide and Gentile ripped the shirt of Zico as he tried to stop the Brazilian ace in the penalty area. But Italy were let off by an earlier offside decision.

Zoff was at his best as Brazil piled on the pressure after the restart, rushing from his line to stop Cerezo and blocking a backheel from Serginho.

Rossi missed a golden chance of making it 3-1 before Falcao, who plays in Italy with Roma, grabbed Brazil's second equaliser after sixty-eight minutes. A deft body swerve deceived three defenders and he planted a shot past Zoff from the edge of the box. But Italy were not to be denied and made the most of their only corner of the game sixteen minutes from time. Conti's corner was headed down to Bergomi and Marco Tardelli's shot was pushed home by Rossi.

Zoff clutched a goalbound header from Junior on the goal-line to foil Brazil's final fling.

POSTSCRIPT

Managed by Tele Santana, the 1982 Brazil side are commonly regarded as the best team never to win the World Cup. Packed with outstanding players like Zico, Socrates, Eder and Junior, the Selecao dazzled with their skills but were cruelly undone by Italy's determined performance.

The Italians would go on to win the tournament, beating West Germany in the final thanks in part to another goal from Golden Boot winner Rossi. Rossi had been banned for two years for his part in a match-fixing scandal, but returned for the Azzuri in May, just in time to lead the successful claim on the world crown.

Paolo Rossi.

World Cup Second Stage Group 3

Italy… (2) 3	Brazil… (1) 2
Rossi 5, 25, 74	Socrates 12
	Falcao 68

Att: 44,000

FA Cup Shocker Bournemouth beat United

IT'S MILTON KEEN

CHERRY-O AS UNITED CRASH

Bournemouth 2 Manchester United 0

Ken Montgomery

Bournemouth's amazing Third Division beach boys produced too many good vibrations for mighty Manchester United – sending the FA Cup holders crashing to spectacular and sensational defeat.

And there was nothing remotely lucky about a performance that earned them their place as top of the shocks.

Milton Graham, a twenty-two-year-old coloured striker, and Ian Thompson, the twenty-five-year-old former schoolmaster who almost joined Manchester City in the summer, handed out the most amazing Cup caning the Old Trafford all stars have experienced in years.

But every man in the Bournemouth side – the Third Division strugglers they call the Cherries – was a hero.

United, who crashed out of the Milk Cup last month to Oxford, must have nightmares about meeting Third Division opposition.

But there was nothing remotely third rate about Bournemouth, whose boss, Harry Redknapp, trains his team on the South Coast sands.

They matched mighty United for muscle. They were United's equal for effort. They showed every bit as much skill as their illustrious opponents – and they finally gave them a lesson in the glorious old art of finishing.

Admittedly, Manchester went into the match with the massive twin disadvantage of being without experienced central-defenders Kevin Moran and Gordon McQueen, both injured.

Mike Duxbury and the eighteen-year-old Scottish debutant, Graeme Hogg, were drafted into their places, and neither looked comfortable.

To add to their troubles, Remi Moses missed the second half, and we had the unusual sight of veteran sub Lou Macari having to play at full-back.

Bournemouth were unlucky to go in at half-time still only level. They made most of the running, and Milton Graham even hit the crossbar with a header just on the tea break.

But he did not have to wait long for compensation.

It came in the sixtieth minute, when the industrious Chris Sulley's right-wing corner was badly missed by Gary Bailey, and Graham swept the ball home.

United were already flying distress signals, and then Ian Thompson drove home a second Bournemouth goal two minutes later.

United boss Ron Atkinson must have realised that the Cup holders were heading for a sensational fall.

Man of the Match: Milton Graham (Bournemouth).

Bournemouth… (0) 2 Manchester United… (0) 0
Graham
Thompson

Att: 15,000

Milton Graham scores the opening goal.

Five All!

FIVERS!

QPR 5 Newcastle 5

John Hall

Gary Micklewhite crowned the fightback of the season as Ranger's Houdini hot-shots came back from the dead to snatch a miraculous point.

Four down at the interval, Alan Mullery's shell-shocked side looked dead and buried as Chris Waddle left them standing with a stunning first-half hat-trick.

But Rangers bounced back off the canvas with a comeback that had the Loftus Road fans reaching for the tranquilisers.

Yet, ironically, Newcastle seemed to have put the result beyond recall with a devastating first-half display. Waddle gave them the start they so desperately wanted, darting to the by-line in the third minute for a perfect cross which was headed home by Neil McDonald.

Then after seventeen minutes, Haddock's pass sent Waddle racing clear of the Rangers' defence and he coolly drew Hucker before sliding the ball into the net.

Rangers could hardly believe it – and a third goal six minutes later seemed to have left them without a prayer. They were again caught napping as Ken Wharton's close-range effort came back off the post for Waddle to score with ease.

Bookings for Stainrod and Wicks underlined Rangers' frustration. But worse was to come as Waddle completed his hat-trick with a stunning twenty-five yarder.

Rangers ought to have been dead and buried. But Gary Bannister's persistence two minutes after the interval suddenly gave them a glimmer of hope.

Rangers' new boy watched in dismay as his close-range header was parried by Carr – but was onto the rebound in a flash to score.

Suddenly, Rangers sensed their chance and they were back in the hunt after fifty-seven minutes when an attempted clearance cannoned past Carr off the unlucky Wharton.

Thirteen minutes later John Gregory reduced the arrears further with a delicate chip, only for Wharton to restore Newcastle's two-goal advantage from Waddle's eighty-fifth-minute cross.

That ought to have been the end, but unbelievably Rangers found new reserves as Wicks rose to head home Micklewhite's cross a minute later.

Even then, the equaliser looked beyond Rangers, only for Micklewhite to pop up dramatically in the dying seconds to snatch the most unexpected of points.

Football League Division One	
QPR... (0) 5	**Newcastle... (4) 5**
Bannister	McDonald
Wharton (o.g.)	Waddle 3
Gregory	Wharton
Wicks	
Micklewhite	

The One and Only

BREWED BY THE NEWCASTLE BREWERIES, NEWCASTLE UPON TYNE, ENGLAND

NEWCASTLE

Newcastle manager Jack Charlton.

Everton Biggest European Night

FINAL TOUCH

EVERTON'S TREBLE IS SO CLOSE

Everton 3 Bayern Munich 1

Alec Johnson

Everton marched proudly towards their treble-chasing dream with one of the fightbacks of the season last night.

The First Division champions-elect, already through to next month's FA Cup final, landed a place in the European Cup Winners' Cup against Rapid Vienna in Rotterdam on May 15th with a gutsy show after going behind at Goodison.

But the club's biggest crowd of the season, 49,476, were stunned five minutes before half-time when Everton conceded their first goal of the competition.

But three second-half goals steered Howard Kendall's men to their first-ever European final and extended their unbeaten run to twenty-four games.

Everton should have got off to a dream start after only four minutes.

Following a free kick, Peter Reid crossed to the unmarked Steven standing only eight yards out, but Steven mishit his volley to send the ball skidding across the face of the goal.

But after thirty-seven minutes the Germans struck.

The fast moving Kogl broke away down the middle. Although goalkeeper Neville Southall did well to block his shot the ball only ran loose for Hoeness to ram home.

Everton's Andy Gray celebrates a goal with Graeme Sharp, Peter Reid and Paul Bracewell in the final.

Everton pushed forward after the restart and within three minutes levelled through top scorer Sharp.

Stevens's long throw was headed on Gray and Sharp glanced the ball in at the far post for his twenty-ninth goal of the season.

Everton took command and Paul Bracewell and Sharp missed chances before Gray scored the second goal in the seventy-second minute.

Another Stevens long throw was mishandled by Pfaff and Gray swept the ball in.

With Bayern committing everyone to attack, Steven sealed the victory with a third.

Afterwards, Gray accused Bayern of having a soft centre.

"They dished it out but were not too happy when they got some stick back," he said.

"It was a physical game, but at the end of it we have beaten one of the best teams in Europe.

"Bayern had only one chance and scored from it. It's an absolutely unbelievable feeling to be going to a European final."

Manager Kendall said: "I have not known many nights like this. Going behind was the last thing we wanted and it gave us a tough job to do."

European Cup Winners' Cup Semi-final Second Leg	
Everton... 3	Bayern Munich... 1
Sharp	Hoeness
Gray	
Steven	
	Att: 49,476

POSTSCRIPT

Everton landed their first (and only) European trophy to date with a 3-1 win over Rapid Vienna. The Merseysiders would go on to win the League but in an unforgettable campaign just missed out on a famous treble, losing to Manchester United in that season's FA Cup final.

Bobby Robson before the kick-off at the Azteca Stadium.

150

1986 Sunday 22nd June

England Play Argentina and God

OUT OF THIS WORLD

ENGLAND ARE SENT PACKING

Argentina 2 England 1

Harry Miller

England yesterday were cheated out of their most important clash with old rivals Argentina, who moved into the semi-finals of the World Cup.

The game we had all waited for with a nerve tingling mixture of eagerness and apprehension ended in bitter disappointment for Bobby Robson's men.

So Argentina have finally got their revenge. They have never considered the one-nil defeat they suffered in the 1966 World Cup quarter-finals as anything other than an injustice.

At the final reckoning they were more fired up for this one than England. The honour of a country that has been second best to England so often needed to be satisfied.

Now England head for home and Argentina go forward to fly the South American flag against a three-pronged European onslaught. They will present a formidable challenge.

Peter Reid was in trouble as early as the fifth minute when he fell clutching his right ankle that made him doubtful until twenty-four hours before kick-off.

He was clearly handicapped and limping heavily when Diego Maradona exploded into one of his devastating runs.

Peter Shilton shakes the other hand, before the kick-off.

The little striker went past three tackles before Terry Fenwick brought him down and was promptly given the yellow card.

From the free kick Maradona drove in a shot, deflected off the wall that Peter Shilton pushed over the bar to safety.

Argentina were comfortable and composed on the ball, but over confidence let England in for the game's first chance after eleven minutes.

Goalkeeper Pumpido got caught outside his area with the ball, Peter Beardsley took it off him and swivelled to drive into the side-netting.

There was danger whenever Maradona ran at England but the defence closed him down well, giving good support and making vital interceptions.

It was clear that we were prepared to hit on the break shoring up the back to give Shilton cover he needed.

England couldn't get enough of the ball to build any attacking football, and Argentina slowly squeezed a grip on the game.

Maradona was behind most of their moves, but England were quick to deal with him.

It was dour, drab football, and one reason was that Glenn Hoddle could not yet find his range to set Gary Lineker free.

When Maradona was pulled down he took the free kick himself and curled the ball just wide of Shilton's left post.

Another free kick by Maradona was deflected over the bar for a corner and when the little man took it himself, Shilton made a plunging two-handed catch.

But again Maradona exploded into life and after another exhilarating run, Steve Hodge miskicked wildly for a corner.

England were able to hold out, but Argentina were quicker and more positive.

England worried Argentina with a free kick that could have spelled danger just before half-time.

Ken Sansom backheeled it and ran on, Hoddle picked him out, Hodge was offside as he ran across and England's first chance of a breakthrough was ruined.

But England were stunned in the fifty-second minute when Argentina went ahead after a definite handball by Maradona.

He begun the move that stretched England at the back, and when he got the ball back, he challenged Shilton – and put his hand up to divert it into the net.

England chased referee Ali Bennaceur of Tunisia all the way back to the centre circle protesting passionately, while the stricken Shilton also indicated that Maradona had fisted it past him.

But there was nothing illegal about Maradona's second goal. He beat three men in an electrifying dribble that took him past Peter Reid, Terry Butcher and Terry Fenwick before slipping the ball past Shilton.

In the eighty-first minute England at last broke through. Substitute John Barnes beat two men, crossed from the left, and Gary Lineker headed his sixth goal of the competition.

Maradona scores, by himself.

Maradona scores with some help from God.

World Cup Quarter-final	
Argentina... (2) 2	England... (0) 1
Maradona 52, 55	Lineker 81
	Att: 114,580

FA Cup Final Classic

THE GRAND FINAL

Coventry 3 Spurs 2

Ken Montgomery

The FA Cup is Coventry's for the first time in their 104-year history. And nobody but Gary Mabbutt could possibly begrudge these Sky High, Sky Blues the sweet scent of success.

The no-hope men from the Midlands won a wonderful, a spectacular, an incredible, a sensational 106th FA Cup final with the help of an own goal by Mabbutt in extra time.

Twice the team with no chance were behind. Twice they growled. Twice the mongrels bit back against Tottenham's kennel of pedigree poodles.

But they deserved to win it. They earned their greatest day since Lady Godiva was doing the business on her horse.

And when poor Mabbutt put his paw in it five minutes into extra time to steer a Lloyd McGrath cross past Ray Clemence, Tottenham were the Crufts Champs who finally had their collars felt. Mark my words, this wasn't Hollywood stuff. Twentieth Century Fox, Metro Goldwyn Mayer – not even Joan Collins – could have produced a saga like this.

It was thrills, spills, action all the way, and the fact that it took an own goal to decide a match where you could hand Oscars to almost every performer, was immaterial.

Tottenham, the raging hot favourites, the peacocks who came strutting out at an amazing 2-1 on to take their eighth FA Cup back to White Hart Lane had their tails in the air after only 111 seconds.

Coventry City and Spurs make their way on to the Wembley turf.

Chris Waddle, one of the sensations of an outrageously sensational afternoon, went bursting through on the right-wing.

He pin-pointed his cross superbly, and Clive Allen, the Footballer of the Year, the Players' Player of the Year, was on the spot to nod his forty-ninth goal of the season.

It wasn't lambs to the slaughter. It was mongrels ready to be put down, we thought. But George Curtis and John Sillett have breathed fire, fury and ferocity into the new-look Sky Blues.

There were only eight minutes on the clock when they were level. Big Cyrille Regis, who at twenty-nine is developing the freshness, the force and the power of a two-year-old, was in on the act.

His first cross was bundled out of the Tottenham box. Dave Phillips's shot was blocked.

The ball bounced clear to Greg Downs. He found Dave Bennett clear on the left-hand side of a congested, confused Tottenham penalty area.

Bennett – Dave, not Tony – did a solo spot that even the American crooner would have been proud of.

He kept his heart at Wembley Stadium. He kept his head. He kept his cool.

But again the see-saw swung Tottenham's way.

There seemed no real problem when the elegant Hoddle floated one of his tempting free kicks into the penalty box four minutes before half-time.

Amazingly, alarmingly, Big Oggie in the Coventry goal, went AWOL. He didn't get near the ball.

Richard Gough did, nodded it on with a back header to Mabbutt and Tottenham were 2-1 ahead.

The referee, a superb Neil Midgeley, credited the goal to Coventry City's captain Brian Kilcline.

Tottenham insist that it was Mabbutt who got the final touch.

In the circumstances Mabbutt should have it because this was the day when we saw the agony and the ecstasy performed by one person – poor Mabbutt.

But nobody can write off Coventry – and by hell, did they prove it. Out they came after their half-time cuppa – or was it a bowl of Pedigree Chum – and off they went straight at the Tottenham jugular.

Keith Houchen scores for Coventry.

In the sixty-second minute, Bennett again found space down the right, his cross was perfection and Keith Houchen – yes you pronounce it like Ouch – was there to make it 2-2.

Nobody in the 100,000 crowd who had paid more than £1.25 million to watch the action in the raw, dared blink or they'd miss out on another memorable moment.

They started extra time with Gary Stevens replacing the ageing Argentine veteran Ossie Ardiles.

And still the majority of a mesmerised audience were convinced that the classy people from Tottenham would put the mongrels from Coventry in their corner – but not a bit of it.

Finally, dramatically, desperately for Mabbutt, but deliriously for Coventry, the winner came.

McGrath ran hard, fast and wide to find himself a place on the right. He had been fed by a superb ball by Coventry substitute Graham Rodger.

A McGrath cross might have been Mabbutt's. It may have

been Clemence's. But Mabbutt put his foot out and put his foot in it.

The cross ricocheted away from Tottenham's punky little defender, agonisingly out of Clemence's reach and the Cup was Coventry's.

It was an eccentric way to win an electrifying football match. But it was deserved.

Tottenham, full of skill, full of arrogance, full of ambition, gave their lot and their lot just wasn't quite good enough.

Waddle produced moments of magic I honestly believed were beyond him.

Hoddle, in his farewell fling for Spurs, gave us moments of absolute elegance.

DID YOU KNOW

This match established a new British gate receipts record of £1,286,737.50p

1988 Saturday 9th April

A Hat-trick aged 17 on his Debut

GEORGE FURY!

KID ALAN K.O. BLOW

Southampton 4 Arsenal 2

Graham Baker

Angry Arsenal manager George Graham warned his players that none of them can count on playing in the Littlewoods Cup final on April 24th.

Graham's shame-faced team of £1,000-a-week superstars were hustled away by their boss after being shot down by a debut hat-trick from Alan Shearer, who gets £35 a week on the Youth Training Scheme.

"I have tried to instil into them that they are all playing for their places," said Graham.

"The first hour highlighted what I have been trying to preach. I thought Southampton gave us a hiding.

"The last half hour we played some lovely football, but it is no use starting to play for your pride when you are 4-1 down.

"This is the worst we have played since I took over. I am just glad it has happened now, with a few games to sort it out before Wembley.

"We cannot afford to relax in any game. The public pay their money and deserve more than that.

"I think it must be difficult to get Wembley out of their minds, but if they think they can just go through the motions they are in for a bit of a surprise."

Arsenal must have felt even more humiliated that their destroyer was a seventeen-year-old kid fresh out of the youth team.

Shearer, who got the call at midday after England winger Danny Wallace failed a fitness test, struck after five, thirty-three and forty-nine minutes. Saints' other goal came from Mark Blake.

Saints deserved to complete the double over the Gunners, despite an amazing own goal by Kevin Bond after ten minutes.

Paul Davis did score an excellent second goal after eighty-two minutes... but it was too late.

POSTSCRIPT.

Shearer went on to play 158 times for Southampton scoring 43 goals before his £3.6 million transfer to Blackburn Rovers. He played 138 times for Rovers, scoring 112 goals. In 1996 he moved "home" to Newcastle United for a world-record fee of £15 million and played 303 times for the Magpies where he netted 148 goals. His England caps numbered 63 with 30 goals scored.

League Division One	
Southampton... 4	Arsenal... 2
Shearer 5, 33, 49	Bond (o.g.) 10
Blake 44	Davis 82

"I canna believe it!"

1988 Wednesday 13th April

Liverpool demolish Forest

KENNY'S BUNCH OF FIVES

TITLE IS ON ICE

Liverpool 5 Nottingham Forest 0

Chris James

Liverpool last night saved the best for last as they turned on the championship style to take another giant step towards their second double in three seasons.

They are now just two points away from clinching their seventeenth League title after destroying their only serious challengers Nottingham Forest, 5-0 in front of an adoring, admiring Kop.

First-half goals from John Aldridge and Ray Houghton put Liverpool on the road to triumph.

And with Gary Gillespie, man-of-the-match Peter Beardsley and Aldridge again adding further goals, it amounted to Liverpool's biggest win of the season.

Liverpool now go to Norwich next Wednesday needing to win to make the title a mathematical certainty, but with their massive advantage in goal difference, a draw would surely be enough to bring the trophy back to Anfield.

After the comprehensive demolition of Brian Clough's kids before a near-40,000 crowd, Anfield boss Kenny Dalglish added: "I think a lot more people than myself are enjoying the way we are playing.

"Now we need two points for the title and we've got six games to get them."

Aldridge, whose brace took his total for the season to twenty-seven added: "The lads were just magnificent."

John Aldridge.

Peter Beardsley.

League Division One

Liverpool... (2) 5   Nottingham Forest... (0) 0
Houghton
Aldridge 2
Gillespie
Beardsley

Att: 39,535

160

1988 Sunday 24th April

Let's Hear It for the Little Guys

TOP HATTERS!

SIZZLING STEIN STRIKES TWICE FOR WEMBLEY DREAM DAY

Arsenal 2 Luton 3

Harry Harris

Two-goal sensation Brian Stein destroyed Arsenal in one of the most breathtaking Cup final finishes Wembley has ever seen.

Stein, the South African-born striker who set this five-goal thriller into motion as early as the thirteenth minute, ended the Gunners' reign as Littlewoods Cup holders with the winner just seconds from time.

Yet it never looked as though the Hatters would enjoy their champagne party when George Graham's team stormed back to take a 2-1 lead late in the second half.

But Luton, kings on plastic at Kenilworth Road, proved they can also play on grass and put aside the misery of losing the Simod Cup final a month ago to Second Division stragglers Reading 4-1.

Luton's first major honour in their ninety-one year history – they lost the 1959 FA Cup final to Nottingham Forest – will be remembered for the spectacular finish.

And not since Alan Sunderland won the FA Cup for Arsenal with a goal five minutes from the end of their 3-2 win over Manchester United, has a Wembley victory been achieved with such a dramatic late goal.

Luton won the hearts of the nation when they kept their nerve and courage to topple the Gunners in a final that started so slowly it was in danger of being one of the most forgettable.

When it burst into life it was almost impossible to keep track of events, which included a hotly disputed penalty that goalkeeper Andy Dibble brilliantly saved.

The amazing finale kept nearly ten million viewers on the edges of their seats watching the most exciting of all the live TV offerings this season.

Those cameras also caught Arsenal's David Rocastle's dive to win the controversial penalty when Mal Donaghy went to make a challenge.

Had Dibble not dived full length to his left to turn Nigel Winterburn's spot kick around the post, Arsenal would have taken an unassailable 3-1 lead and kept the Cup.

Luton produced several match-winning performances on the day. Dibble for his penalty save, denying Alan Smith when he was clean through and chipping another Smith header on to the bar when Arsenal were buoyant. Brian Stein for the sting that floored the Gunners, Steve Foster for serving up a delicate touch to create Stein's first goal, and for his usual defensive domination.

Again it looked as though Graham had conjured up a winning formula when he sent on Martin Hayes for Perry Groves and the Gunners turned a 1-0 deficit into a 2-1 lead. But it was Luton sub Ashley Grimes' penetrating run to the by-line and his devastating cross that created Stein's last-gasp winner.

Then there was Danny Wilson's brave equaliser and the dynamic aerial menace of Mick Harford, until injury forced him off. It also was hard to believe that Ricky Hill was playing his first game in four months after recovering from a broken leg.

Hill's inclusion was a gamble that paid off for manager Ray Harford, who, like Graham before him, has won the Littlewoods Cup in his first season in management.

The Gunners had strolled to Wembley as clear favourites, having conceded just one goal and netted fifteen en route to the final.

But the thirteenth minute proved unlucky. Paul Davis fouled Kingsley Black and the free kick by David Preece searched out Harford, and the presence of three Arsenal players – Kenny Sansom, Tony Adams and Groves – could not clear the danger.

Foster produced a surprisingly delicate touch with a half-volleyed pass to send Stein clear and he slid his shot wide of John Lukic.

Arsenal went behind to an Ian Rush goal a year ago only to storm back, but this time they were strangely disjointed in the first half.

Luton might have taken a two-goal lead when Harford burst clear of Gus Caesar, pulled back his cross and Stein's header brought Lukic's best save of the game in the fifty-first minute.

The younger Stein, Mark, came on for the injured Harford and almost scored immediately. He rounded Adams but chipped over Lukic and the bar.

Then came the Gunners' stirring fightback with two goals in three minutes.

A Davis centre broke loose and sub Martin Hayes stretched to prod the ball over the line.

Hayes was involved again as Michael Thomas supplied a square pass for Smith to compose himself before shooting into the corner.

After the penalty drama Luton hit back. Brian Stein's shot was blocked and Danny Wilson stooped to head the equaliser with just six minutes left.

Extra time looked inevitable. But in the last minute Adams was guilty of a foul on Mark Stein that earned him a lecture from referee Joe Worrall.

The Gunners failed to clear the free kick and Grimes rounded Kevin Richardson before crossing for the lethal boot of Stein to stroke home the winner.

Littlewoods Cup Final

Arsenal... (0) 2	Luton... (1) 3
Hayes 71	B Stein 13, 90
Smith 74	Wilson 84
	Att: 95,732

Luton's finest hour?

The Crazy Gang's Big Day

WIZARD WOMBLES

DONS DESTROY KENNY'S DREAM

Liverpool 0 Wimbledon 1

Ken Montgomery

Football fairytales do still come true – and yesterday those wonderful Wombles of Wimbledon proved it.

Bobby Gould's blue and yellow heroes turned Wembley and the 107th FA Cup final into an outrageous rags-to-riches romance.

And it was all down to a goalkeeping Goliath called Dave Beasant and a Bachelor of Science named Lawrie Sanchez.

They were the men who wrecked red-hot Liverpool's hopes of making history by pulling off the double for the second time in three years.

Liverpool, the team with all the pedigree, can have no complaints. They were beaten deservedly by a bunch of mongrels who had more belief in themselves than we, the critics, ever had.

And as the celebrations continue at Plough Lane for a club who were not even in the Football League eleven years ago, the two super Dons who made it all possible should be given the freedom of the borough.

Hero No. 1 was Lawrie Sanchez, the twenty-eight-year-old who joined Wimbledon for a mere £30,000 from Reading three years ago.

Big Lawrie is a Bachelor of Science in business studies. He did the business alright in the thirty-sixth minute of an amazing final. Little Dennis Wise cleverly glided a short free kick to the near post when Liverpool were expecting the traditional Wimbledon long ball.

Sanchez met it perfectly, and with one deft flick of his head the ball floated beyond a bewildered Bruce Grobbelaar.

The miracle was happening.

Hero No. 2, Captain Marvel goalkeeper Dave Beasant, was determined the fairytale script was in no danger of being re-written.

Beasant, twenty-nine, nine years at the club and making his 351st consecutive appearance for these incredible Dons, was playing the starring role in Wimbledon's soccer upset of the century.

You could see it would be Big Dave's day as early as the twenty-fifth minute when Peter Beardsley pushed a glorious through ball to Ray Houghton.

The shot was firm but it ricocheted off Beasant's legs. He gave it a second nudge as it rolled up his arm and then scooped the ball one-handed off the line.

Time after time, even though Liverpool looked a shadow of their awe-inspiring best, big Dave was in magical mood. He had a day he will remember for the rest of his life.

We expected John Barnes, a double Footballer of the Year, to be the jewel in the Wembley crown. Or perhaps Peter Beardsley. Maybe even Ray Houghton or Alan Hansen or Steve McMahon.

But the guy who glittered gloriously was Beasant.

The climax came in the sixty-first minute when full-back Clive Goodyear was harshly judged to have tripped John Aldridge as Liverpool menaced the Wimbledon penalty box.

Aldridge, who has scored all of his eleven spot kicks this season, was expected to square the issue and set Kenny Dalglish's stormtroopers on their way to the inevitable.

But Beasant threw his 6ft. 4in. frame to his left and pawed the ball to safety.

It was the first penalty miss in a Wembley FA Cup final, and the despairing Aldridge trudged off to the substitute's bench.

Wimbledon had a team of diamonds. Little Dennis Wise

gave everything and more; Andy Thorn kept his calm in a match which could have exploded; and tireless Vinnie Jones battled ferociously.

Referee Brian Hill should have been much more stern with Jones, Wimbledon's tough nut defender, in the ninth minute when he steamed in on Steve McMahon from behind.

It was a day of strange decisions. A day when the result was nothing short of sensational.

Yet it might have been different had Mr. Hill not been quite so quick with his whistle in the thirty-fourth minute.

Hansen fed Beardsley into the Wimbledon penalty box and the England striker, whose £1.9 million transfer fee is double what the Dons squad has cost, was blatantly fouled by Thorn.

But Beardsley stumbled through the foul, regained his composure and slotted the ball past Dave Beasant – only to turn and see the referee disallow his goal and award Liverpool a free kick outside the box instead.

Yet in all of the Anfield despair at missing out on the double, their dour Scottish manager Kenny Dalglish hardly got the sympathy other losers regularly receive.

His superstars just didn't do it on the day. The super Wombles rolled up their sleeves, growled like tigers and got on with the business of creating a sensation.

Their fans were outnumbered in a Wembley crowd of 98,203 by at least 10-1. But bless the Liverpool faithful. Five minutes from time they were still imploring their heroes: "Walk on, walk on, with hope in your hearts."

They were left to walk alone, lonely, beaten, bewildered by that unglamorous team of bighearted heroes who had the time of their lives on a sunny day at Wembley.

Unbelievable!

FA Cup Final

Liverpool... (0) 0	Wimbledon... (1) 1
	Sanchez 36
	Att: 98,203

Liverpool Denied Their Eighth Title Win in a Row

THE GREATEST STORY EVER TOLD!

GRAHAM NIGHT OF TRIUMPH

Liverpool 0 Arsenal 2

Harry Harris

Arsenal last night pulled off a soccer miracle to deny Kenny Dalglish a place in history.

Dalglish was bidding to become the first manager to win the double twice, following his triumph three years ago.

Instead, in one of the most dramatic climaxes to any championship season, the Gunners proved they are worthy champions.

The North London glory boys stole the title from the clutches of the FA Cup winners with almost the last kick of this sensational and traumatic season.

Michael Thomas, who had earlier missed a golden chance, made no mistake with an injury-time goal that put the two giants level on points and goal difference, with the Gunners taking the title by scoring more goals.

George Graham's team seemed to have thrown the championship away at least twice in recent months, but their

Arsenal players form a wall. Left to right, Michael Thomas, David Rocastle, Kevin Richardson, Alan Smith, Perry Groves and Steve Bould.

seventy-three goals outstripped Liverpool's sixty-five.

It is ninety years since two teams last went into the final match each with a realistic chance of taking the title.

And this time the exhilarating climax was shared by millions of TV viewers. ITV are paying £50 million for an exclusive contract and they got their money's worth as Arsenal clinched their first title for eighteen years – the last time their current manager Graham was in their line-up.

At 10.19 last night, Graham walked off the Anfield pitch with the championship trophy firmly in his grasp, writing his name in the Highbury Hall of Fame just as he always wanted to do.

Graham had joined in Arsenal's lap of honour as some of the Arsenal players broke down with tears of joy, while some Liverpool players wept in despair.

Many Liverpool supporters stayed on the Kop to sportingly applaud the new champions as Arsenal fans sang "You'll Never Walk Alone" and triumphantly chanted "Champions".

They also mockingly bellowed "Boring, boring Arsenal", sarcastically turning on everyone who has accused them of negative tactics.

The Gunners have won the championship by scoring eight more goals than Liverpool, with Graham putting the emphasis on entertaining football.

Arsenal dropped home points against Sheffield Wednesday, Millwall, Nottingham Forest and Charlton, but really looked to have thrown away the title with self-inflicted wounds – squandering five points in their last two Highbury games, losing to Derby and drawing with Wimbledon.

When Liverpool thumped West Ham 5-1 to send the East Enders down, no one gave the Gunners a prayer of winning by two. They had not scored two goals at Anfield since 1974, when Alan Ball scored twice and Liam Brady once. They had lost their last seven First Division games here.

There were more omens in Liverpool's favour. John Aldridge and Ian Rush had never been on a losing side in partnership, while goalkeeper Bruce Grobbelaar had not been on a losing side in twenty-eight games this season, keeping thirteen clean sheets.

It was stacked against Arsenal, but there was an amazing spirit within the camp. They actually believed they could pull it off. Graham said before the game he was very optimistic. David Rocastle revealed that none of the players were frightened by the daunting task ahead of them.

Even without two of their best players, Brian Marwood and Paul Davis, Arsenal clinched their ninth championship with a remarkable performance.

They strode out with each player holding a bouquet which they presented to the fans.

The Gunners were determined not to leave Anfield empty-handed, while Liverpool were favourites to add the title to the FA Cup they had won at Wembley by overwhelming Everton in another exciting match.

Graham began the game sitting in the directors' box alongside his chairman Peter Hill-Wood and vice-chairman David Dein.

By the start of the second half he was down on the bench. The Gunners might have taken an early goal when a cross from Thomas was misjudged by Grobbelaar and Steve Bould's header was goalbound until Steve Nicol headed it over his own bar.

Although Bould was recalled as Graham gambled by reinstating his sweeper system, Arsenal were always ready to attack.

A breakthrough goal after fifty-two minutes, thirteen seconds put the championship on a knife-edge.

Liverpool skipper Ronnie Whelan fouled Rocastle and Nigel Winterburn's free kick was headed into the corner by Alan Smith.

Liverpool fervently protested that Smith's twenty-fifth goal of the season – his twenty-third in the League – should not have counted because referee David Hutchinson had raised his arm for an indirect free kick and the Liverpool camp were insistent that Smith had not got a touch.

Dalglish was on the touchline as both sets of players surrounded the referee in his consultations with the linesman.

But the goal was given and suddenly Arsenal took total command. Thomas stabbed a seventy-fourth-minute chance created by Kevin Richardson straight at Grobbelaar from close range, and Arsenal's hopes seemed to falter.

Graham pulled off Paul Merson, bringing on Martin Hayes. A few minutes later he brought off Bould, substituting him with Perry Groves.

Richardson was booked for a foul on Ray Houghton and

Tasting victory.

Rocastle was shown the yellow card for dissent.

Houghton was put in the clear by Aldridge with just seven minutes to go, but blasted his shot over when he could have picked his spot.

As the minutes ticked away Arsenal were so much on the offensive that John Barnes was forced to play centre-half, heading out a Groves cross as Liverpool were pinned back in their own half.

Liverpool broke and Beardsley and Aldridge faced just one defender. But Aldridge, with twenty-nine goals this season, lacked the technique to control the ball as it bounced away from him.

As the game spilled into injury time Barnes robbed Arsenal skipper Tony Adams, setting off on a dribble which never came off. Lukic threw the ball out to Lee Dixon, his long ball was knocked on by Smith and there was Thomas in the clear.

Thomas had so much space and time it seemed to take an eternity before he struck the championship-deciding shot past a helpless Grobbelaar.

Aldridge dropped to his knees, Barnes lay on his back and David O'Leary was in tears. The Gunners' longest-serving player had finally tasted championship success.

The Barclays title comes to London and no one in the 41,718 crowd or the millions watching at home can begrudge the Gunners their greatest triumph.

POSTSCRIPT

Arsenal's dramatic, last-minute victory came just a matter of weeks after one of British football's darkest days, when ninety-six supporters were killed in the Hillsborough disaster. The Gunners' triumph provided much of the basis for Nick Hornby's book *Fever Pitch*, later turned into a hit film and seen as a turning point in the game's fortunes.

Barclays League Division One	
Liverpool... (0) 0	Arsenal... (0) 2
	Smith 52
	Thomas 90
	Att: 41,718

City Thrash United

UNITED ARE A SHAMBLES

OLDFIELD LEADS THE GOAL RUSH

Manchester City 5 Manchester United 1

Bill Thornton

Manchester United's multi-million pound rebuilding programme was reduced to rubble by their heaviest derby drubbing for nineteen years.

Despite the eleventh hour loss of injured Bryan Robson, United arrived at Maine Road full of hope after scoring five themselves the previous week.

They left with faces to match the famous red jerseys, City having made a mockery of the difference in valuation between the teams.

Going into the game with only one win and five league goals to their credit, Mel Machin's men could hardly believe the gaps in the sad and sorry United defence.

Admittedly there were moments when the home back line also didn't look too clever.

But there was never a period when United threatened to escape from the hole which they had themselves dug.

A minute of madness began the slide for Alex Ferguson's costly collection shortly after shocking crowd scenes had resulted in the teams being led off the field by referee Neil Midgely.

After just three minutes, fighting fans behind Jim Leighton's goal spilled onto the pitch.

The players were off for eight minutes and United certainly seemed worse for the break. Defensive lapses quickly helped City to two goals in fifty seconds.

First Gary Pallister looked anything but a £2.3 million centre-back as he failed to clear David White's right-wing cross. David Oldfield lashed home the loose ball.

Then Trevor Morley robbed Mal Donaghy on the edge of the penalty area. His shot was brilliantly saved by Leighton, who also kept out White's following effort.

But the ball fell kindly back to Morley, who gleefully fired his first goal of the season.

Andy Hinchcliffe cleared off the line from Pallister's overhead kick and Gary Fleming did likewise from the head-bandaged Brian McClair as the Reds frantically sought to claw their way back.

But they were dead and buried by Ian Bishop's first goal for City in the thirty-fourth minute.

Sent away on the right by the outstanding Steve Redmond, Oldfield gave Pallister the slip before crossing for Bishop to head home spectacularly.

Mark Hughes did reduce the arrears with a crashing volley in the fifty-first minute and so nearly got his head to Viv Anderson's cross three minutes later. But these were only flickering moments of hope in a shambling display.

Oldfield grabbed his second in the fifty-seventh minute after Leighton had parried Paul Lake's shot.

Hinchcliffe completed the rout, charging upfield to power home a header from White's cross.

Football League Division One

Manchester City... (3) 5 Manchester United... (0) 1

Oldfield 9, 57	Hughes 50
Morley 10	
Bishop 35	
Hinchcliffe 60	

Att: 43,246

There Are No Easy Cup Semi-finals

WEMBLEY HERE WE COME

PALACE PRINCES

Crystal Palace 4 Liverpool 3

Harry Harris

Crystal Palace stole the hearts of the nation with a mixture of furious fact and fantasy in probably the biggest FA Cup semi-final upset in history.

Palace's pulsating passage to their first ever FA Cup final appearance was little short of a miracle – an even bigger shock than Wimbledon's Wembley defeat of Liverpool two years ago.

Liverpool humiliated Palace 9-0 at Anfield last season and there was even a video released of that remarkable goal glut.

So who would have thought it remotely possible that Palace could have beaten Liverpool in the FA Cup semi-final after that?

But not only did Palace win one of the most important games of the season, they also thoroughly deserved it.

Not even Liverpool, now denied their dream of winning the double, could deny palace their most glorious day in their history.

Remarkably it was little known Alan Pardew, a £7,000 buy from Vauxhall-Opel League side Yeovil Town, who finally sealed Liverpool's fate after precisely 109 minutes and six seconds.

Steve Coppell, a candidate for manager of the season, raced on to pitch at the end in jubilation then remembered the defeated and sportingly turned back to shake the hand of Liverpool boss Kenny Dalglish.

The Cup that Liverpool won on such a tide of emotion a year ago was torn from their grip by a Palace side now persuaded by Coppell that the impossible was possible.

Perhaps he remembered that he had never lost an FA Cup semi-final in three chances as a player with Manchester United.

Now, the joy of this incredible victory belongs to Palace and the chief architects of the win Mark Bright and Andy Gray, celebrated by running over to their jubilant fans, where they lost their shirts in the kissing and the hugging.

Palace's triumph lies easily alongside other great wins this year, such as Buster Douglas' victory over Mike Tyson, England's success in the West Indies and Norton Coin's defeat of Desert Orchid.

At the end of this epic struggle the Eagles had landed at Wembley.

In fact the Liver Birds of Liverpool have rarely had their feathers ruffled more than they did yesterday.

The first live TV coverage of an FA Cup semi-final may well prove to be the best.

Liverpool, three points clear in the First Division with a game in hand and with only one defeat in their previous twenty-three games, began true to form by dominating Palace with their calm, controlled possession.

Steve McMahon released a perfect pass, with Ian Rush timing his burst to perfection.

As the Palace defenders naïvely stepped forwards with hands raised in a line appealing for offside, Rush executed a delightful chip over the advancing Nigel Martyn for his twenty-third goal of the season.

But Rush lasted only another sixteen minutes before being forced to retire with a painful hip injury and Liverpool lost their momentum.

At the start of the second half, Dalglish used his second substitution with Barry Venison replacing Gary Gillespie who suffered a groin injury.

Ian Rush is a little premature.

Ian Wright with a helping hand from Steve Bruce in the final at Wembley which Palace drew 3-3 with Manchester United, Wright scoring twice, only to lose the replay 1-0 to a Lee Martin goal.

And it took Palace just sixteen seconds to spark Villa Park into an electrifying atmosphere with an equaliser.

Gillespie's absence was even more significant as Liverpool were destroyed at the heart of their defence, their vulnerability exposed like a raw nerve.

Liverpool were stung by the speed of Palace's equaliser.

As they kicked off the second half, McMahon's line attempt to find Steve Staunton on the wing failed as full-back John Pemberton intercepted and sped off.

He found a gap through the Liverpool defence and his cross was struck at the far post by John Salako and blocked on the line by Staunton. But Bright struck a full-blooded volley that struck McMahon on the head as he stood on the line and ricocheted into the roof of the net.

Palace skipper Geoff Thomas was denied a goal as keeper Bruce Grobbelaar saved on the line, but the underdogs took the lead after sixty-nine minutes through defender Gary O'Reilly.

Pemberton's free kick caused panic in the centre of the Liverpool defences as the ball dropped for O'Reilly to crack it past Grobbelaar.

With just nine minutes remaining and Palace believing that Wembley was in sight, McMahon smashed an equaliser after a smartly-worked free kick, and two minutes after that Liverpool were ahead.

Pemberton was harshly adjudged to have tripped Staunton and John Barnes converted the penalty.

But Liverpool threw the semi-final away with just two minutes remaining as Grobbelaar's attempted punch failed and as Staunton attempted to head off his own goal-line, Gray roared in for the equaliser.

Brave Palace might have won it in normal time when Andy Thorn, a Cup final winner with Wimbledon over Liverpool, thumped a header against the bar from Gray's curling free kick.

The year of the underdog was complete in the 109th minute when Gray's corner was flicked on at the near post by Thorn, and Pardew headed it over the line.

Every one of the Palace team were heroes in their own right and none more so than Martyn, Britain's first £1 million goalkeeper.

The former coalyard clerk from Cornwall was signed to Bristol Rovers after Perry Suckling's confidence was shattered after conceding those nine goals at Anfield.

Martyn's best of a series of saves was from Barnes's close range header in the 115th minute that he somehow scrambled to safety. His former manager Gerry Francis believes he is already the best of the bunch chasing Shilton's England Jersey.

Even without his injured twin striker Ian Wright, Bright was a handful for a Liverpool defence that simply couldn't cope with Palace's dead-ball set plays.

And Pemberton typified the Palace approach. His only claim to fame was having attended the same school as England's David Platt and playing with the Villa marksman for their local club Chadderton.

Now Pemberton, such an influence in Palace's first two goals is following Platt to Wembley via Rochdale and Crewe. He cost Palace just £60,000.

Defensive kingpin Thorn has been convinced for some time that his team's name is on the Cup – just like he felt it was for the Dons two years ago.

FA Cup Semi-final

Crystal Palace... (0) 4	Liverpool... (1) 3
Bright	Rush
O'Reilly	McMahon
Gray	Barnes (pen)
Pardew	
(At Villa Park)	

Att: 38,389

A Little Tear Falls

WE HAD THE WHOLE WORLD IN OUR HANDS

CRUEL DEFEAT FOR BOBBY'S BRAVES

England 1 West Germany 1

Harry Harris

England had the world in their hands – and then saw it cruelly snatched away in an agonising penalty shoot-out here last night.

An historic place in the World Cup final was denied England as Stuart Pearce and then Chris Waddle missed penalties in a nail-biting semi-final showdown against West Germany.

England's World Cup campaign had ended in tears and heartbreak in the magnificent Stadio Dell Alpi in the cruellest way possible.

But the whole nation can be proud of this England team of heroes as they reached out for the summit of world football brimming full of guts, passion and commitment.

And Gary Lineker declared afterwards: "We can certainly go home, with our heads high."

It was so near, yet so far for Bobby Robson's brave warriors as they came desperately close to taking their place in the final against Diego Maradona's world champions.

England began the World Cup playing the sort of football that was condemned as stone age against the Republic of Ireland – but they finished it with a brand of sophistication that few believed they possessed.

England not only matched, they, at times, outplayed the Germans – the best team in the tournament – and might have won.

For a manager who has been the most vilified in English football, Bobby Robson will be a proud man today.

Few expected England to reach the World Cup semi-finals and when they got there they graced the occasion.

The tears flowed as Pearce, in particular, seemed inconsolable.

Pearce hung his head in anguish and shame as his fierce penalty – England's fourth – struck goalkeeper Bodo Illgner on the legs before Olaf Thon converted and then Waddle blasted his kick over the top.

It was a sad, senseless way to go out but England are not alone in suffering as the whole Italian nation has grieved since Tuesday when they lost in similar fashion to Argentina.

But that sadness must not mask how close England came to success.

England lost to Maradona's Hand of God goal four years ago in Mexico and this time by rights should be heading for Rome to avenge that in the fourteenth World Cup final.

Instead Robson's ninety-fifth and final match as England manager won't be the biggest occasion in world football.

It will be the consolation prize of the play-off for third place against Italy in Bari on Saturday.

Robson will reflect with mixed feelings about this match and despite the defeat, it will fill him with deep satisfaction that his side almost beat West Germany.

Now Franz Beckenbauer will be aiming to become the first player and manager to win a World Cup, in the repeat of the final of four years ago.

West Germany have reached their third successive final, a record sixth final appearance, playing in a record sixty-seventh game in World Cup Finals, surpassing Brazil.

England could not have taken on a more experienced country, or a tougher challenge in such an important match.

With Mark Wright needing a special protective covering because of six stitches in a wound around his eye, Robson altered his defensive formation and started with skipper Terry Butcher as sweeper and Wright and Des Walker as the man-to-man markers.

Once again Wright and Walker were superb at the back and Paul Gascoigne was marvellous in midfield, England's biggest success of the World Cup.

Gazza was reduced to tears by Brazilian referee Jose Ramiz Wright in the eighth minute of extra time when he was shown the yellow card for his foul on Thomas Berthold.

It meant that Gazza would have been ruled out of Sunday's final.

That proved academic, but at the time Gazza visibly wobbled and he was shaken so much that he could hardly play for the next few minutes.

England were also denied a penalty when Waddle was brought down in the box by sweeper Klaus Augenthaler.

And it was Waddle who rattled the inside of the post in the 105th minute with a rasping left-foot drive.

England rode their luck against Cameroon in the quarter-final, but in Turin theirs ran out.

England had fallen behind to a fortunate opening goal, when Thon placed a short free kick to Andreas Brehme, whose shot took a wicked deflection, off the foot of Paul Parker.

Peter Shilton, a couple of yards off his line, got his hand to the ball as he fell backwards but couldn't stop it going in.

Shilton made two vital saves before Gary Lineker came to England's rescue once again.

With just ten minutes of normal time remaining and Steve Bull warming up, Parker's long searching pass embarrassed the West German defence.

First Juergen Kohler made an unconvincing contact and Augenthaler's challenge on Lineker failed as the Spurs striker took full advantage.

He sped past the German defence and fired a terrific left-foot shot into the corner.

In extra time, Gazza regained his composure after his booking and he powered up the right-flank only to be kicked up in the air by Brehme, who was booked.

Platt headed into the net from Waddle's free kick but was caught offside.

Then as the game drifted towards penalties, with just three minutes to go, Guido Buchwald curled a shot against Shilton's left-hand post.

At the end of extra time, England's third successive two-hour stint in this tournament, Gazza collapsed to the floor knowing his World Cup was over no matter what happened.

The thousands of England fans in the stadium tried to lift his spirits by chanting "We love you, Gazza."

The Spurs star waved back to them but was in floods of tears and the England manager consoled him, deciding that he was in no fit state to be involved in the penalty shoot-out.

Lineker, Beardsley and Platt completed the nerve-wracking task of scoring from the penalty spot, but Brehme, Matthaeus and Riedle converted theirs.

Pearce, a fierce striker of the ball, has a reputation of being deadly from the penalty spot, but his penalty failed and then Thon converted his.

The tension intensified for Waddle and his nerve broke as he fired over. England had battled to the last – but in the end it just wasn't enough.

World Cup Semi-final

England... (0) 1	West Germany... (0) 1
Lineker 80	Brehme 60
Aet. 90 mins 1-1	
West Germany win 4-3 on pens	
	Att: 62,628

1991 Sunday 14th April

The First FA Cup Semi-final to be Played at Wembley

G-WHIZZ IT'S SPURS

GARY AND GAZZA OUTGUN ARSENAL

Spurs 3 Arsenal 1

Terry Venables' "Gazza Gamble" paid off in spectacular style as Spurs destroyed Arsenal's double dreams and gloriously salvaged their own season of disaster.

Venables bravely opted to start with Gazza just thirty-five days after the player's groin operation and Spurs stormed to an FA Cup final date with Brian Clough's Forest on May 18th.

The footballing megastar, valued by Italian club Lazio at a world record £8.2 million, created breathtaking havoc inside the opening ten minutes. vVenables might have played safe and put Gazza on the bench. Instead the irrepressible and cheeky talents of England's World Cup hero were unleashed on Arsenal from the very start with unbelievable consequences.

Gazza cracked up after an hour under the strain of such a quick comeback from surgery and inevitably had to come off. But this impact had already been devastating on favourites Arsenal.

Gazza's wicked free kick from nearly forty yards and his George Best like magic to prise open the Gunners' mean machine defence for Gary Lineker's opening strike put Spurs into a startling two-goal lead before his man-to-man marker Michael Thomas knew where he was.

Arsenal demonstrated their formidable commitment and passion with a spirited fightback, but Lineker's killer goal will haunt skipper Tony Adams and England goalkeeper David Seaman. Lineker's pace took him wide of Adams, but his angled drive was within Seaman's grasp. Yet despite getting both hands to the shot the most expensive goalkeeper in the world at £1.3 million could only guide it into the corner.

Any Cup hangover on the Gunners' title bid will become evident in just three days when they confront Manchester City at Highbury to protect a five-point advantage over Liverpool.

The double was pretty high stakes for the Gunners. But for Spurs, their very survival was on the line in this historic first Wembley FA Cup semi-final.

Spurs may be bust financially, but they are now bursting with the hope of Venables' first trophy after more than three and a half years at the club.

Even more important than the quest for silverware is the need for cash and they can hear the sound of coins flooding in to the coffers to ease the panic of the Midland Bank's £10 million overdraft.

Sell Gazza? Unthinkable!

Spurs' passage to the FA Cup final may save the club – and Gazza. Even when Gazza was removed from centre stage he couldn't keep still on the bench, leaping to his feet to conduct the chorus of cheers from the Spurs' section of the near 78,000 crowd.

Now Gazza will play in the first Cup final of his young career. One could argue that he has almost single-handedly taken Spurs back to Wembley having made such an impact in all the previous rounds.

Little wonder after having such an influence on Spurs' destiny, he raced around Wembley for a personal lap of honour, then led his team-mates around the famous stadium. He even came back for an encore and was the last to disappear down the tunnel!

Even two goals by England's most formidable current marksman, Gary Lineker, couldn't overshadow Gazza yesterday.

It was a first-minute tackle on Anders Limpar that led Arsenal straight into trouble. Limpar was left seething by Vinny Samways' challenge, with full-back Pat van den Hauwe kicking Limpar while he was on the ground.

In the fifth minute Limpar got his revenge with a late

challenge on Paul Stewart – and the consequences for the Gunners were dire. Gazza lined up for his shot from such long range that Arsenal hardly assembled a protective wall.

But Gazza let rip and the speed of his shot deceived Seaman, who got a hand to it but couldn't stop it cracking against the back stanchion. George Graham wanted young David Hiller to chaperone Gazza around Wembley, but had to recall Thomas for the job. Gazza demolished Arsenal's defence with the trickery of a double first-time flick. First he clipped the ball to Paul Allen and on its return he flicked it between Steve Bould and Thomas to put Allen in the clear on the right-flank.

With Gary Mabbutt lurking at the far post, Arsenal striker Alan Smith cut out Allen's cross, trying to control it on his chest. But it bounced away and that was all the invitation the predatory Lineker needed.

Spurs' master goalscorer reacted a split second sooner than Adams to poke the ball past Seaman from close range.

Smith scooped a shot high over the bar from Nigel Winterburn's cross before Arsenal hauled themselves back into the game with just seconds ticking away before the interval.

Justin Edinburgh's header out of defence was picked up by Smith and spread wide to full-back Lee Dixon.

Keeper Erik Thorstvedt left his line and then retreated as Smith outjumped Mabbutt to head into the corner.

Graham, who had been shaking his head in dismay at his team's first-half performance, stoked up his team during the interval and afterwards the chances flowed for the Gunners.

Spurs were wilting under the siege and with signs of a Gazza limp, he was replaced on the hour by Nayim.

After another weak finish from Limpar, he was taken off to be replaced by Perry Groves. There was always a suspicion that Arsenal would find a way through until Mabbutt's pass gave Lineker possession. Samways, who wore Gazza's number eight shirt with distinction in his injury absence, made a perceptive dummy run. Lineker took full advantage to wrap up the Cup-tie with his seventy-sixth minute goal.

Samways got a standing ovation, led by his manager, when he was replaced near the end by Paul Walsh. He shared the honours alongside the likes of Paul Allen and Mabbutt.

Paul Gascoigne leads the celebrations.

FA Cup Semi-final

Spurs... (2) 3   Arsenal... (1) 1
Gascoigne 5   Smith 45
Lineker 10, 76

Att: 77,893

The Welsh Do It Again

ARSENAL DIDN'T WANT TO KNOW

"WE CRAVED VICTORY MORE THAN THEM."

Wrexham 2 Arsenal 1

Old-stager Gordon Davies helped plunge crisis-club Arsenal into deep despair, and then accused them of lacking desire.

Wrexham's former Chelsea and Fulham favourite reckoned the Gunners panicked themselves into the biggest upset in FA Cup history.

Leading by Alan Smith's forty-fourth minute goal, Arsenal failed to kill off the plucky, but limited Fourth Division team.

And Wrexham's mixture of callow kids and old soldiers snatched two goals in two minutes late in the game to shatter the League champions' season.

Grey-haired Davies, now thirty-six, and on the brink of quitting the game here to manage a Norwegian Second Division team, twisted the knife when he said: "I was surprised by the way they let it slip.

"I thought they were going to be more professional but they seemed to lack desire to win the game. They seemed to settle for 1-0 and then played it like a training match.

"We've got a team of youngsters and two old men, and perhaps we wanted the win more than they did.

"A few of them were complaining to each other all afternoon."

They are words that should make Arsenal boss George Graham wince. In the space of seven months, his once-proud Gunners have become goners. Highbury champs have turned chumps.

This barely believable defeat to the team who finished bottom of the whole league last May blew up Arsenal's one remaining route out of their season of gloom.

The alarm bells started ringing when they crashed out of the Rumbelows Cup with barely a whimper to relegation-haunted Coventry in late October.

Then came a shattering early exit from the money-spinning European Cup as Benfica cruelly exposed their limitations.

Hopes of retaining their First Division title have vanished after picking up only nine points out of the last twenty-seven.

Now Wrexham – a club who would have been playing in part-time soccer this season but for the decision to increase the size of the League, have handed out the final humiliation.

This was the season when Arsenal, committed to a multi-million pound rebuilding scheme, desperately needed to figure among soccer's glittering prizes.

Graham couldn't suppress his bitter disappointment saying, "I came into football expecting the highs and the lows. There was quite a few highs as a player and since I became a manager, but this has been the lowest.

"When you start the season in four competitions and are not in any of them by January it's a big blow to your season."

But Graham refused to publicly condemn his players saying, "I've no complaints about them it was a good all-round performance. We lost a game we should have won. We just didn't capitalise on the chances.

"There's a very thin line between success and failure. They got a mysterious free kick and scored from it. If they hadn't have got it I think we would have finished comfortable winners. But that's football."

Graham must have been alarmed by the lack of confidence, killer instinct and discipline – especially in the final half hour. The turning point came in the eighty-second minute when David

Steve Watkin.

FA Cup Third Round

Wrexham... (0) 2	Arsenal... (1) 1
Thomas 82	Smith 44
Watkin 84	

O'Leary was pulled up for a push on the edge of the area.

Mickey Thomas struck a powerful free kick into David Seaman's top right-hand corner to cancel out Alan Smith's opener. Two minutes later a Thomas pass gave Davies the chance to steal a yard on O'Leary.

He turned the pass inside where Tony Adams fluffed his attempted clearance and rookie striker Steve Watkin hooked the ball home to guarantee his place in FA Cup folklore.

Victory was sweet for thirty-seven-year-old Thomas whose goal embellished a performance of energy and skill. His career has spanned twenty years, more than 700 games and eleven clubs, but he was still the best player on the pitch.

"That's the most crucial goal of my career and I owed Arsenal for a couple of defeats."

Fastest Ever Yellow Card

CARRY ON CLOGGING!

CHELSEA BOSS GIVES JONES GREEN LIGHT FOR WEMBLEY

Chelsea 1 Sheffield United 0

Harry Harris

Vinnie Jones has been given the go-ahead to "carry on clogging" all the way to Wembley by manager Ian Porterfield.

Porterfield not only excused Jones for an ugly tackle that got him booked within three seconds of the start – the Chelsea boss also reckoned it was Vinnie who steered the Blues into the quarter-finals.

Porterfield said: "It was almost worth the booking because it proved how much we wanted to win.

"United were on a high and came here to turn us over. Unless our attitude had been right, they would have done so."

Jones broke his own record for the quickest ever booking – previously five seconds – when he clattered into Dane Whitehouse.

Porterfield said: "Vinnie went in to win the ball and didn't. If it had been any other player no one would say a word – because it's him, it's been blown up."

United's John Gannon was another swift booking for a tackle on Clive Allen, then Jones set the fists flying by holding on to the ball after United won a corner.

After that referee Keith Burge called together captains Andy Townsend and Brian Gayle and told them to cool things.

Burge said: "I booked Jones for a late foul tackle and Gannon for a late challenge. I had to tell the two captains to calm it down.

"The game started at such an explosive pace I had to react to stop it getting out of hand.

"Both captains promised to co-operate and get hold of the game. They had to otherwise somebody would have been sent off. Fortunately the players responded and it calmed down.

"I don't like booking players but sometimes you have to."

Jones' former manager, Dave Bassett, quipped: "I've seen Vinnie booked quicker – but only by 0.5 seconds! He did it once at Wimbledon, but at that time he didn't even worry if the fellow had the ball." But United skipper Gayle said: "I've never seen anything like the first five minutes. When the Jones boy is playing, anything can happen.

"He was up against his old club, so everyone was hyped up. I've just been talking to him. He's been blowing cigar smoke in my face and talking about the quarter-finals of the FA Cup.

"The referee told Andy Townsend and myself to calm things down. The referee did well. A lot of other referees would have sent somebody off and not taken the trouble to discuss it first with the captains. That's why we knew we had to get hold of the players."

Once again Jones' brand of football comes under the microscope. But Porterfield insists: "He gets criticism, but not from Chelsea Football Club. When I bought him from Sheffield United I explained to him the disciplines we have within the club, and the way we approach things.

"He's been a credit, as far as I'm concerned on the pitch. He has performed consistently, his attitude has been great, his enthusiasm infectious.

"If he plays badly or well you can still be assured he will give everything. It's about time people started writing good things about him.

"He's a winner. He wants to succeed."

There was no degree of reprimand whatsoever from Porterfield. That illustrates the intensity of Chelsea's drive towards the FA Cup final – at all costs.

But Vinnie was on the receiving end in the second half – and that could land United's Carl Bradshaw in trouble with the FA.

Although the referee apparently did not see it, TV replays spotted Bradshaw swinging a punch at Jones and missing – but catching the Chelsea man with his head.

Graham Stuart sent Chelsea into the last eight with a neatly worked solo goal in the twenty-fourth minute.

Left to right, Brian Deane, Graham Stuart and Vinnie Jones.

FA Cup Fifth Round

Chelsea... (1) 1	Sheffield United... (0) 0
Stuart 24	

*The Inaugural Champions
League Season*

WILKO'S HERR-OES!

AGONY FOR LEEDS AS GERMANS HIT THEM ON THE BREAK TO LAND EURO K.O.

Leeds 4 Stuttgart 1

Harry Harris

Salute Leeds United for one of the most magnificent failures of all time in the European Cup.

The English champions dropped to their knees in exhaustion after a performance of true grit that came so agonisingly close to overturning a 3-0 first-leg deficit.

Brilliant goals, inventive attacking football, but frailty in defence finally ended Leeds' continental campaign at the first hurdle.

Nevertheless nothing should detract from a display that the nation can be proud of. Gary Speed, Gary McAllister, Eric Cantona and Lee Chapman collected the goals as Leeds had enough chances to have doubled their tally.

Stuttgart produced sufficient opportunities on the break, but the one that decided the tie will haunt Leeds. As they threw themselves into a whirlwind of attacking football Leeds were caught out with Andreas Buck's thirty-fourth minute angled drive flying across goalkeeper John Lukic and into the net.

It was a crying shame, for the technique and the creativity – so often purported to be exclusive rights of the continentals –

Six weeks earlier Leeds had won the Charity Shield, beating Liverpool 4-3, with a hat-trick from Eric Cantona seen here holding the shield.

were exhibited by a courageous English side.

The two Scots in midfield, Gordon Strachan and McAllister, oozed class and control, while Cantona was a potent cocktail of power and magic.

Leeds had held the highly-rated German champions for just over an hour in the Neckerstadion a fortnight ago before falling apart with three goals conceded in the final half hour.

Manager Howard Wilkinson preached patience, but in reality he wanted an early goal and he got it from Speed in the eighteenth minute. Strachan's pass was headed down by Cantona perfectly for Welshman Speed, who struck it brilliantly on the volley, and the ball flew past keeper Eike Irnmel.

But when Stuttgart equalised on the night through Buck it needed a second phenomenal effort – and incredibly Leeds provided it. Once again Strachan crossed, causing panic in the Stuttgart defence and the experienced skipper Guido Buchwald shoved Chapman over in the box. McAllister made no mistake from the penalty.

Then in the sixty-fifth minute Cantona's muscular build enabled him to shrug aside a defender and lob the keeper from close range. Leeds struck the bar before they collected their fourth in the eightieth minute. Strachan took a corner and with Stuttgart stuttering Chapman scored with a near-post header.

What a frantic final ten minutes! The hearts were pounding and Wilkinson's pulse rate racing as Leeds narrowly failed to become the first British club to recover a three-goal deficit.

And the Stuttgart manager Christoph Daum had another narrow escape as he was leaving the stadium – his team bus colliding with the back of the main stand. Daum and several Stuttgart officials were showered with splintered glass when a window was shattered, but no one was seriously hurt.

European Cup First Round Second Leg	
Leeds... (2) 4	**Stuttgart... (1) 1**
Speed 18	Buck 33
McAllister 38 (pen)	
Cantona 66	
Chapman 80	
Agg. 4-4. Stuttgart win on away goals	*Att: 20,457*

The Lowest Ever Premier League Attendance

3,039

DONS IN DISASTER

Wimbledon 1 Everton 3

Nigel Clarke

The Wimbledon fairytale looks almost dead and buried. The final curtain is about to fall on the Crazy Gang.

Just 3,039 fans, the lowest ever recorded attendance for a Premier League or First Division match, mourned their relegation disaster last night.

The club are losing £5,000 a day and are £1.5 million in the red. It seems that they are at last doomed after eight years in the spotlight.

They have no crowd, no money, no atmosphere. Only hope keeps them going. At kick-off time there were just three supporters standing on the Holmesdale Road terracing that holds 7,000.

And midway through the match club owner Sam Hammam walked behind the goal to stand alone there, a forlorn figure in the rain. It could now signal a clear-out if the Dons look doomed to go down.

John Scales, Warren Barton and Robbie Earle, all valued at £2 million, could be put up for sale before the March transfer deadline.

Manager Joe Kinnear trudged off in despair at the final whistle as Everton killed them off with three goals in eleven minutes.

He said: "You just have to put your arms round the players, give them a kiss, and tell them to battle on. We have to re-

group, be even closer to one another and dig in.

"I won't have a word said against them, but all I can say is that Howard Kendall must have been the luckiest man in the world to go in at half-time with the score 0-0.

"Everton should have been dead and buried by then but we missed our chances yet again. There are eighteen matches left, fifty-four points to go for and we'll be in there battling.

"It's strange, the same team beat Liverpool only two weeks ago, but psychologically our lack of a crowd must go against us."

But it took an amazing incident to breathe fire and life into two teams who have already met five times this season, including three goalless draws.

Snodin fouled Wimbledon's Roger Joseph and immediately Vinnie Jones rushed in to intervene.

Jones has a history of bad blood against Everton and was twice sent off at Goodison Park after incidents involving Kevin Ratcliffe and Peter Reid.

This time though referee Keith Hackett incredibly took no names as seventeen players were involved in a bad tempered blow-up.

Then Tony Cottee stepped into the act to show the kind of finishing that may yet keep him at Goodison.

The £2 million striker, who has been out of the side for so long, struck in the sixty-second and seventy-first, minutes after errors by Dean Blackwell, and then saw Snodin add the third.

Wimbledon had only their pride to play for and when John Fashanu got a goal back it was with a looping header that saw goalkeeper Neville Southall stranded in his goalmouth.

Kendall said: "Cottee did well. We've had talks about his future and I'd like him to stay at the club."

FA Premier League

Wimbledon... (0) 1	Everton... (0) 3
Fashanu 75	Cottee 61, 71
	Snodin 73
	Att: 3,039

1996 Wednesday 3rd April

North West by North East

STAN-DING OVATION!

Liverpool 4 Newcastle 3

Steve Millar

A look to the skies gave us a sighting of the brightest comet this century and an eclipse of the moon.

But back down on earth at Anfield we were privileged to see something that was out of this world. Football not of our planet, with enough shining stars to send Patrick Moore into overdrive.

It was an unbelievable, mind-blowing experience that will live with me and the other privileged spectators forever. We sat in awe of two teams challenging for the championship of England.

But I would have made them both kings of the universe. I have never been so elated and totally drained after ninety minutes of football that saw Liverpool finish winners.

But how the hell can you describe Newcastle as losers? That's an insult. True, the defeat leaves rivals Manchester United in the driving seat at the top of the table and will be a much needed pick me up for flu ridden boss Alex Ferguson.

But who can count out either of these two great sides from getting their hands on the three foot high piece of silverware next month?

This famous ground has seen many memorable matches, but none of the 40,000 jammed noisily into Anfield could have expected the action that was to follow before the cameras had rolled on this greatest show on earth.

It was like buying a ticket for a pleasure flight and finding yourself upgraded to Concorde. We were treated to a supersonic flight of fancy which included seven goals of breathtaking magnificence that deserve equal billing.

The first took our breath away after ninety-seven seconds and the last found the net two minutes into injury time to keep the crowd behind long after the final whistle with endless choruses of "You'll Never Walk Alone".

They came thick and fast these seven wonders of the soccer world. The first went to Robbie Fowler as he ended a marvellous move

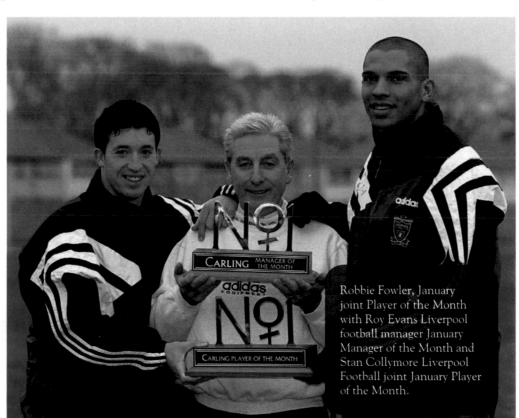

Robbie Fowler, January joint Player of the Month with Roy Evans Liverpool football manager January Manager of the Month and Stan Collymore Liverpool Football joint January Player of the Month.

he'd begun far out on the right. Jamie Redknapp took over the challenge to sweep the ball out to Robert Jones lurking on the left of the box.

His deft touch dropped to Stan Collymore who stepped past Steve Watson to deliver the perfect cross for Fowler to head down into the net.

But in the ninth minute Newcastle were level. Faustino Asprilla looked to be facing the immovable object of Neil Ruddock when he found the ball at his feet and causing no apparent threat. Suddenly he nutmegged Ruddock and pulled the ball back for Les Ferdinand to swiftly turn and shoot home through the despairing hands of keeper David James.

Phew! You didn't think there was any more to come but oh, how we were mistaken as Newcastle blazed into the lead after fourteen minutes.

Ferdinand, with his back to goal, controlled the ball in one brilliant moment and then sent it swerving into David Ginola's path in the next. The fantastic Frenchman out-paced Jason McAteer and then hammered into the net for his first goal since January 2nd.

We then had to wait another forty minutes for the fourth goal of the night but we were kept well entertained in that period with some gobsmacking football.

The next strike came courtesy of Fowler who leapfrogged England striker Alan Shearer with his thirty-fifth goal of the season.

Steve McManaman embarked on a weaving run with Philippe Albert backing off for safety.

But just when the Belgian thought the danger was over McManaman picked out Fowler who drove home the equaliser and then finished up in the back of the net after a bellyflop on the turf.

Sixty seconds later Newcastle were back in the lead and looking a safe bet to claw back Manchester United's three-point lead. Peter Beardsley linked with Robert Lee, who sent Asprilla on his way with Liverpool desperately appealing for offside.

Referee Mike Reed would have none of it, allowed play to continue and the Colombian cockily screwed the ball in past stranded keeper James.

The Newcastle bench erupted. They thought it was all over. But it wasn't. McAteer sent a swerving ball into the area and beyond keeper Pavel Srnicek and there was Stan Collymore to prod the ball home to make it 3-3.

And with referee Reed adding on a couple of minutes at the end Collymore struck to dig the dagger deep into Keegan's heart.

Wise old head John Barnes did all the hard work in shielding the ball and laying it across for Collymore to steady his nerves before drilling the ball into the bottom corner to lift the lid off Anfield. Seven magnificent strikes and too many chances to mention. We had a couple of Redknapp thunder-bolts, a McManaman left footer which was deflected over the bar.

A push from Barnes on Asprilla in the box that looked a penalty and then a John Scales header which hit Fowler on the line and bounced away from the danger zone.

We saw, too, Srnicek push away a Barnes pile driver and then somehow beat out a snap shot by Redknapp.

In fact we witnessed everything that is good about our national game.

POSTSCRIPT

Often described as the "game of the 1990s", this seven-goal thriller encapsulated Newcastle's season – brilliant one minute, horribly vulnerable the next. These inconsistencies undermined the Magpies' effort to win their first title in sixty-nine years. Their commanding lead at the top had been whittled away by Manchester United and this defeat was pivotal in the Geordies eventually missing out on the big prize.

Incredibly, Liverpool won by the same scoreline in the same fixture the next season.

FA Carling Premiership	
Liverpool... (1) 4	Newcastle... (2) 3
Fowler 2, 55	Ferdinand 10
Collymore 68, 90	Ginola 14
	Asprilla 57
	Att: 40,702

Kevin Keegan Newcastle United's manager salutes fans at the end of the 1995-96 season.

Shilton's 1000th game

SHILTS – MIRROR SPORT SALUTES A SOCCER LEGEND 1966-1996

NOW GIVE ME THE CHANCE TO BE A BOSS AGAIN

Leyton Orient 2 Brighton 0

Mike Walters

They rolled out the red carpet for Peter Shilton's millennium party yesterday but forgot to provide the old boy with an electric blanket.

At this time of year Help the Aged often stress the importance of ensuring that the elderly are well insulated against the cold.

But in the biting chill of Brisbane Road, forty-seven-year-old Shilts – the grand old man of English football – shivered like an outpatient from a hypothermia ward. And apart from the scriptwriters' scheduled clean sheet, nothing would have been more welcome for the England goalkeeping legend on his 1,000th League appearance than a piping hot cup of tea afterwards.

If Shilts was looking to mark his unrivalled achievement by effecting a lock-out, he could not have picked more accommodating opposition than Third Division bottom-dogs Brighton.

So feeble were the crisis-hit South Coast club that they deprived him of touching the ball for twenty-four minutes, save a couple of expertly-taken goal kicks.

And by the time Shilton was rescued from his battle against frostbite, his most emphatic contribution was better suited to Orient chairman Barry Hearn's boxing stable.

A favourable ricochet gave Stuart Storer a rare sniff of goal – Shilton's right hook to clear connected with the Brighton striker's nose, too. Shilts is itching for another managerial post, two years after he was bombed out of Plymouth when his personal finances descended into chaos.

He said last night: "In the back of my mind I would love to go back into management. There was a lot of indifferent publicity at Plymouth, if you go into my record there, I think you will see I did a good job.

"I just hope someone out there will give me a chance and build on my experience for the future.

"Coming to Orient and completing 1,000 League games has been like a fairytale for me, especially as I've been so close for quite a while. I was fed up waiting around on the bench after a few managers at higher levels had shown some confidence in me.

"I felt I might get the odd game in the Premiership, but it didn't happen and I have to prove to people I can still perform.

"I haven't set a deadline for carrying on as a player, but I would have to look closely at any opportunities to become a player-manager for someone at the back end of the season."

Brighton scarcely threatened to spoil Shilton's big day and he said: "I could have done with marking the occasion by making a couple of spectacular saves. As it turned out, it was more a case of keeping your concentration in the high wind and the low sun."

Peter Shilton and Gordon Banks who he replaced at Stoke in 1974.

Shilton's only serious worry was finding a removal van big enough to transport all his awards home to the Midlands last night.

Hearn's programme notes opened with the words: "Without wishing to overstate it, today is a monumental day in the history of football." And for once you were inclined to believe in Hearn's land of hype and glory.

Uncle Baz is the type of salesman who could fetch the same price for an MFI wardrobe as an antique Edwardian tea chest. But he didn't need to overdose on the sales patter to attract

7,944 fans – double Orient's average home gate – to this celebration of soccer's most celebrated antique.

At 11.59 a.m., Shilton emerged for the pre-match kick-in – an exercise infinitely more demanding than keeping Brighton at bay – to a warm ovation. And when the teams formed a guard of honour nearly half an hour later, the old fossil trotted out to the strains of a six-piece fanfare and 1,000 balloons released into the East London sky.

There were endless presentations from ex-World Cup final ref Jack Taylor, Football League secretary David Dent, Hearn and the Brighton Supporters Club. But the formalities were a good deal less interminable than the ninety minutes of largely one-sided scuffling.

For the record, the issue was settled by two-goal Orient skipper Dominic Naylor, a player Shilton once signed on a free transfer for Plymouth Argyle.

On the final whistle, Shilts raised his arms aloft in triumph, while the rest of us breathed heavy sighs of relief.

And The Legend emerged half an hour later to admit: "The main objectives today were to win and keep a clean sheet, so I'm pleased to have achieved both of those.

"Now I'm going to go home, crack open a couple of bottles of champagne with the family and enjoy a nice plate of roast beef or a Chinese takeaway.

"To be honest I've been a bit surprised by the amount of fuss this game has caused – and I've had quite a few faxes from people within the game, which was nice. In the end, I was a bit overwhelmed by the atmosphere. I've played in front of bigger audiences, but this was special.

"I'm not finished yet, which can't be bad for a lad who started on £8 a week as an apprentice at Leicester thirty-two years ago. And it was nice that Dominic, a player who cost me nothing at Plymouth, got both of the goals."

As Naylor prepared to bury his conclusive spot kick in the sixty-fifth minute, some were chanting for Shilton to take it. "Crikey, I didn't know that," he said later. "To be honest, we had enough on our plate today coping with the pressure of live TV coverage without taking penalties as well."

POSTSCRIPT

Shilton went on to play another five matches, resulting in a grand total of 1,005 League games, before finally retiring at the age of forty-seven. The goalkeeper also holds the record for England appearances – 125 in total.

Having lost their Goldstone Ground to developers, Brighton pulled off a last-day miracle at the end of this season to avoid dropping out of the Football League, thanks to a dramatic 1-1 draw away to Hereford.

Shilts displaying his safe pair of hands, back in the day.

Football League Division Three

Leyton Orient... (0) 2	Brighton... (0) 0
Naylor 57, 65 (pen)	

1998 25ᵗʰ May

Into The Valley

CURBS' VALLEY OF DREAMS

CHARLTON BACK IN BIG TIME

Charlton 4 Sunderland 4

Mike Walters

Alan Curbishley has pulled off the kind of miracle Eileen Drewery can only dream about by muscling in on millionaires' row with a fistful of petty cash. And in Charlton`s finest hour their manager even extracted from them a performance as rich in substance and quality as Wembley can have seen.

When they bulldoze the venue of legends next year, and not before time, Curbishley's name will be synonymous with the richest entertainment since a white horse left its hoof-marks on the hallowed lawn seventy-five years ago.

Clive Mendonca's stunning hat-trick will go down as the most priceless treble beneath the twin towers since Geoff Hurst delivered the Holy Grail in 1966.

And in years to come, goalkeeper Sasa Ilic will wonder how on earth he managed to emerge from the mountain of delirium which engulfed him seconds after his decisive save settled the penalty shoot-out which left Wearside awash with tears.

Ilic raced off clutching the match ball after he saved Michael Gray's weak penalty after thirteen successful kicks in the shoot-out.

Mendonca, Steve Brown, Keith Jones, Mark Kinsella, Mark Bowen, John Robinson and Shaun Newton had all been faultless against Lionel Perez.

And Ilic had already been beaten from twelve yards by Nicky Summerbee, Allan Johnston, Kevin Ball, Chris Makin, Alex Rae and Niall Quinn before he pounced on Gray's effort.

Such escapology was once the preserve of Lennie Lawrence, the last Charlton manager to rub shoulders with elite when times were so hard the Official Receiver padlocked the gates and The Valley was overrun by weeds.

In those days Charlton were as homeless as the down-and-outs in Cardboard City up the line at Waterloo.

Like unwanted itinerants they were forced to park their caravans and Portakabins outside Selhurst Park or Upton Park.

And Lawrence would sustain Charlton's dreams with ten bob to spend and outrageous brinkmanship. But look at them now. Not only is The Valley reopened and refurbished, but they can afford to shell out on a new set of Wembley suits. With matching waistcoats, for Pete's sake.

And Curbishley, whose squad cost him only £21.7 million to assemble, can bask in the glory of a fixture list that once again includes Manchester United and London derbies more appealing than a tiff over the garden fence with Millwall.

In vogue now is a refreshing brand of resolute, fearless soccer which is sure to cause long tailbacks in the Blackwall Tunnel from August.

None of this, of course, will be of the slightest consolation to Sunderland, who played a worthy part in the match Lawrence described as "the most gripping play-off final of all time and possibly the greatest match in Wembley's history."

Wearside's big day out was burdened from the outset by the North East's impoverished record at the famous old stadium for the last twenty-five years.

Since Ian Porterfield's winner, Jim Montgomery's acrobatics and Bob Stokoe's war dance in a trilby in 1973, the place has been a graveyard for twelve sides from the Tees to the Tyne.

And for forty-five minutes, Sunderland served up dreary, witless scuffling in the unhappiest traditions of the last quarter of a century. Their monotonous diet of mortar shells towards 6ft. 4in. Quinn was woefully predictable and they were second best in midfield.

Cheer up Peter Reid? Sunderland's daydream believers were so wretched they couldn't pass the salt.

And Charlton, South London's most lovable spendthrifts since Del Boy and Rodders were at large in Peckham High Street, needed only a modicum of efficiency to prevail.

Mendonca's twenty-sixth goal of the season after twenty-three minutes, an assassin's finish from Mark Bright's flick, was the least they deserved before the interval.

At that stage, Charlton's motley collection of old sweats and corner shop bargains looked much too streetwise for the Rokermen, and there was little hint of the thrills to follow.

Reid's pep talk must have contained more pyrotechnics than the pre-match fireworks because Sunderland, stranded in neutral, suddenly found overdrive on the gearbox.

Five minutes after the restart Summerbee's near-post corner caught Charlton napping and Quinn stooped to conquer with an emphatic header.

Then skipper Ball won a 50-50 aerial duel with Keith Jones and sent Kevin Phillips scampering through the Addicks' rearguard to lob the advancing Ilic.

It was Phillips' thirty-fifth goal of term and took him past Brian Clough's club post-war record of thirty-four in a season. He used to clean Alan Shearer's boots at Southampton and, four years ago, Phillips was stacking TVs for a day job and turning out for non-league Baldock Town.

It is a travesty of justice that he won't be going head-to-head with Shearer at the Stadium of Light.

For Phillips, the contest would last only another fifteen minutes before he retired hurt, nursing an assortment of bruises reserved only for the most elusive strikers.

But for the rest of us the pot was only just coming to the boil. After seventy-one minutes, Keith Jones' ball over the top picked out Mendonca, who took it exquisitely in his stride to restore parity and make it 2-2.

Just sixty seconds later, however, Charlton jubilation was stifled in 34,000 throats and once again the cloth cap ruled. Lee Clark crossed from the right, Danny Mills missed out at the far post and Quinn had time to load the chamber, cock the firing pin and pull the trigger on Ilic at his near post.

Roker sub Daniele Dichio, replacing the stricken Phillips, missed a yawning chance to score with his first touch and, just five minutes from the Premiership gateway, keeper Perez joined him in the stocks.

The out-of-contract Frenchman, for whom Wembley was almost certainly his farewell to English football, flapped at John Robinson's corner, got nowhere near it, and Richard Rufus sent this astonishing match into extra time with his first-ever goal.

By now both defences were too tired to batten down the hatches. A whole season's work was reduced not so much to who would crack first, but who would crack more often.

Eight minutes into the encore, Summerbee gave Sunderland the lead for the third time when his fifteen-yard shot, from Quinn's assist, fizzed past Ilic.

Now, surely, it was safe for Bryan Robson and Kenny Dalglish to unfurl the welcome mats and greet their neighbours' return to the big time.

Mendonca, a Sunderland supporter when he was still in short trousers, had other ideas.

Before Charlton had time to be consumed by despair and exhaustion, he had turned smartly on to Steve Jones's cross and completed a devastating hat-trick.

Not even Mendonca could wreak any more havoc before the beta-blockers came out, pacemakers were adjusted and the issue went to that cruellest of last resorts, the penalty shoot-out.

Unkind as they may be, but penalties were good enough to separate Brazil from Italy in the 1994 World Cup final.

And now they have cost Sunderland the chance to complete a reversal of fortune in which last season's three new tenants in the Premiership swap places again with the teams they unseated.

Gray will forever be haunted by Ilic's sprawl to intercept his daisy-cutter, but he need not chastise himself.

As Roberto Baggio will tell him, if penalties can decide a World Cup final they are good enough for Wembley.

The difference, of course, is that you don't get as much excitement as this in a World Cup final – not without Russian linesmen, at any rate.

Football League One Play-off Final

Charlton ... (1) 4

Mendonca 23, 71, 103
Rufus, 85

Sunderland... (0) 4

Quinn 50, 73
Phillips 58
Summerbee 99

Aet. 3-3 after 90 mins. Charlton win 7-6 on pens.

Att: 77,739

After seven years in a state of disrepair Charlton moved back to The Valley in 1990.

1999 26th May

The Greatest Ever Comeback?

TREBLE YELL FOR KING FERGIE

SHERI AND SOLSKJAER SEAL DREAM

Manchester United 2 Bayern Munich 1

Harry Harris

Alex Ferguson's never-say-die troops made one of the greatest ever comebacks to lift the biggest prize of all.

Manchester United went into injury time a goal down to a dominant Bayern Munich but amazingly scored twice in stoppage time to win the Champions League. Fergie's two inspired substitutes Teddy Sheringham and Ole Gunnar Solskjaer both struck from corners to turn the game on its head.

Bayern had hit the woodwork twice in the second half, which would surely have put the game beyond even Ferguson's men. But you have to hand it to United as they claimed an unprecedented treble... they never know when they are beaten.

After thirteen trophies in thirteen years at Old Trafford, twenty-nine trophies in his managerial career, Ferguson now has the one he really wants – the European Cup.

But surely not even the Nou Camp Stadium has ever seen a fairytale finish like this.

And United did it against a team with as much, probably even more, confidence than their own.

After sweeping all before them on the domestic front, the Germans were in no mood to roll over.

In fact after just six minutes Mario Basler beat Peter Schmeichel with a twenty-yard free kick.

The Danish goalkeeper, playing the final game of his glorious United career, was suddenly reduced to the role of bystander when Basler cracked his shot past a crumbling defensive wall.

The ball flew into the far corner with Schmeichel expecting a curler over the wall. It might be hard to accept but justice was served because Ronny Johnsen's challenge on Carsten Jancker looked to have started fractionally inside of the penalty area and carried the powerful striker well into the box after Alexander Zickler hooked the ball into his path.

But Italian referee Pierluigi Collina awarded the free kick two yards outside of the area. Of course the Germans didn't complain. Basler picked his post to perfection instead.

Without inspirational skipper Roy Keane and the influential Paul Scholes, the most crucial area for patched up United was always going to be midfield. Ferguson made his mind up immediately after the FA Cup final, where Beckham played in central midfield after Keane's

198

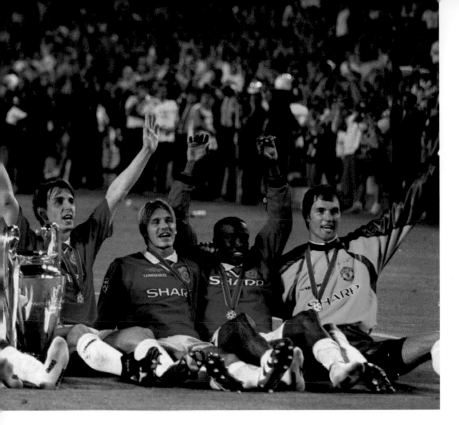

early injury, that the England man would play inside.

But the team's competitive edge suffered by bringing Beckham in from the wings, even if he still showed his footballing pedigree with some devastating long-range passes. The first picked out Ryan Giggs after just seven minutes and later in the half he set Andy Cole racing away into the area.

The energetic Beckham also cropped up on the right-wing, and from one cross Dwight Yorke got a near-post touch which was knocked away by keeper Oliver Kahn.

Cole scuffed a shot, Giggs produced a weak header after a promising rapid counter-break and Ferguson finished the half arms folded in frustration on the touchline. He couldn't wait to produce one his infamous half-time blasts.

But most significantly Ferguson needed to alter his tactics in order to give strikers Cole and Yorke some genuine chances.

For the second half Ferguson dispatched the same side, but it would only be a matter of time before he made changes.

The veteran sweeper Lothar Matthaus was outstanding for Bayern. With his tactical intelligence he was picking and timing his runs with alarming regularity right through the heart of Manchester United's midfield.

There was a moment when Jesper Blomqvist missed the target early in the second half to give United fresh impetus as their momentous support got behind them.

Something like 55,000 fans travelled from England and even though the Germans also had a massive contingent most of the noise came from the English fans.

For the first time the Champions League final was contested by two clubs who were not their country's champions. Both had finished second in their leagues.

Jancker threatened to break through the United rearguard in the first minute after the restart only for Johnsen to make a fine saving tackle. United still searched for an equaliser and Samuel Osei Kuffour did well to intercept Blomqvist's pass intended for Cole before Johnsen headed harmlessly over from a corner.

Markus Babbel then went down in the United box as he went for a corner claiming he had been shoved, but Collina was unimpressed and play went on.

Sheringham finally arrived in place of Blomqvist in the sixty-sixth minute, with Bayern also making a change. Zickler hobbled off to be replaced by Mehmet Scholl.

In the seventy-second minute Stefan Effenberg flashed a long-range effort just wide. Three minutes later he was so close to finding the net. His clever lob looked destined to beat Schmeichel, but the giant keeper just stretched high enough to fingertip the ball over the bar.

A dazzling fifty-yard burst by Basler then almost set up a stunning second. He found Scholl whose delicate chip came back off the post and into Schmeichel's arms.

With the game opening up Ferguson sent on Solskjaer for Cole and within a minute he brought a diving save from Kahn. As United pushed forward they left gaps, and Jancker's stunning overhead kick came crashing back down off the bar. But you can't write-off United, and their two late strikes will go down forever in footballing folklore.

Champions League Final

Manchester United... (0) 2	Bayern Munich... (1) 1
Sheringham 90	Basler 6
Solskjaer 90	
	Att: 90,000

City – The Return to the Big Time

ROYLE HEROES MAKE IT CITY OF MIRACLES

MAINE MEN IN ANOTHER GREAT FIGHTBACK

Gillingham 2 Manchester City 2

Mark McGuinness

Okay, so it wasn't exactly the treble, but for each and every Manchester City fan at Wembley, it felt every bit as good.

A year after the lowest point in this proud club's history, City are back in the First Division, and a long-overdue resurrection appears to be underway.

A game of breathtaking drama ended up in the most sensational victory Wembley has seen since well, probably last season's First Division play-off final between Charlton and Sunderland.

People may have thought Manchester United were dead in last Wednesday's Champions League final against Bayern Munich, but they don't know the meaning of the word compared to their city neighbours.

There were forty-five seconds of normal time left yesterday with Joe Royle's men two-nil down and apparently without a prayer. But football being the strange and unpredictable beast that it is, forty minutes later they were in the First Division and their fans were ready to drink London dry before draining whatever alcohol they could get their hands on all the way up the M1 and M6.

Goals out of nowhere from Kevin Horlock and Paul Dickov brought the game into extra time, and the resulting penalty shoot-out win turned Wembley into a sea of delirious sky-blue.

It has probably been a rough week for most City fans. Seeing your closest and most hated rivals achieve football history is one thing, but having them rub your noses in it for the past five days must have been all the more painful.

And we all know how horrifically immodest United fans are. No, this required instant action by City. They had to rapidly make some headlines of their own, if for no other reason than to remind the rest of the world that there is another team in Manchester.

But when the gauntlet was thrown down, they responded wonderfully. The bravery shown by their team when faced with a footballing Mount Everest was surpassed only by the volume and never-say-die spirit of their brilliant supporters. Football fans are forever being patronised by correspondents of the game, but City supporters truly are special.

Oasis songwriter Noel Gallagher was asked before kick-off what he was most looking forward to about the game. He said: "Knowing we can't get relegated is a wonderful way to be for a City fan at the end of the season."

That just about sums the club up. Let us now hope that almost a decade of slow decline can finally be consigned to history, and this monumental victory can prove to be the catalyst for a new dawn.

City were denied a blatant penalty in the second minute when Shaun Goater's flick was clearly handled in the area by Barry Ashby, but the otherwise excellent referee Mark Halsey missed it and Gillingham survived.

The main threat for City appeared to be through the sweet right foot of winger Terry Cooke, who not so long ago was challenging David Beckham for a place in the United first team. The best chance of the first half came when his beautiful cross landed perfectly on the head of Horlock, whose header was brilliantly saved by Vince Bartram.

City should have scored twelve minutes later when Michael Brown crossed, Richard Edghill nodded down, but Andy Morrison could not connect at the far post.

City started to assert themselves in the second half, but there were signs, especially from Andy Hessenthaler and Carl Asaba, that the Gills could be dangerous on the break. With ten minutes left, Asaba played a lovely one-two with Paul Smith before rifling a shot past Nicky Weaver into the corner.

But the drama was only beginning. Five minutes later Asaba brilliantly back-heeled the ball into the path of Robert Taylor, who slotted the ball under the City keeper from just outside the area.

This would normally have been the cue for the losing fans to desert Wembley en masse. But only a few started to trickle out, and the rest geared themselves up for the final five minutes of screaming their team on.

They were rewarded with an extra half an hour. With a minute to go, Goater was tackled as he was about to shoot, but the ball rebounded to Horlock, who slammed it home through a sea of legs.

Instantly, the Football League official on the sideline informed us through his electronic board that there was to be five minutes of injury time, a luxury most of us thought was reserved only for Manchester United.

Three minutes later Horlock headed down a long ball on the edge of the area to Goater, who found Dickov, and the Scot blasted into the top corner from fifteen yards.

There were precious few chances in extra time, although City should have scored when Horlock's cross was headed straight at the keeper by Dickov. It was to be penalties.

It seemed that Royle had had his men practising, because while Horlock, Cook and Edghill all scored, Gillingham's Smith and Adrian Pennock missed while John Hodge converted the only successful spot kick.

It was left to Robert Taylor to score the penalty that would keep his side in it, but his effort was blocked and half of Wembley erupted.

Spare a thought for Gillingham this morning. They played as well as they could have hoped, and in manager Tony Pulis they have one of the best young coaches in the game.

But Wembley is a place for winners, and when they needed it most, City were able to call upon the reserves of the human spirit that make their arch-rivals United so special.

ON THIS DAY
Prime Minister Tony Blair prepared to send 50,000 troops into Kosovo as the NATO led assault against Serbia continued... Lottery operator Camelot revealed a drop in sales... England crashed out of the cricket World Cup.

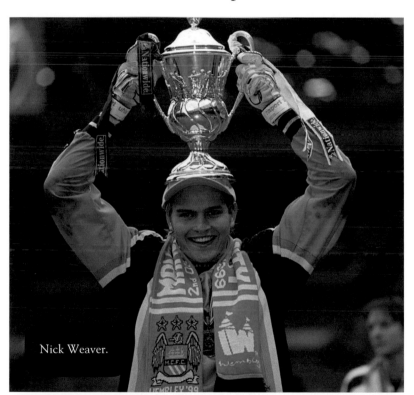

Nick Weaver.

Nationwide Division Two Play-off Final	
Gillingham... (0) 2	Man City... (0) 2
Asaba 81	Horlock 89
Taylor 86	Dickov 90
Aet. Man City win 3-1 on pens.	
	Att: 76,935

*The Greatest Comeback in
FA Cup History*

KING KEV'S MIRACLE

THREE GOALS DOWN WITH 10 MEN? NO PROBLEM FOR KEEGAN'S CITY

Spurs 3 Manchester City 4

Martin Lipton

Kevin Keegan's man management has never been in doubt, but last night the little man excelled himself by inspiring the greatest comeback in FA Cup history.

Sky blue dreams of an Old Trafford FA Cup showdown with Manchester United were seemingly shattered by a first-half horror-show at White Hart Lane, with Keegan watching in disbelief as his shocking side were cut apart by fantastic goals from Ledley King, Robbie Keane and Christian Ziege.

Then the City boss was left dumbstruck when Joey Barton was sent off by referee Rob Styles for a second yellow card for persistent dissent after the official had blown for half-time.

To make matters even worse for the former England coach, top scorer Nicolas Anelka limped off with an apparent groin strain which could keep him out for two weeks.

It looked like another devastating night for Keegan, but whatever he said at half-time clearly worked a miracle as his team suddenly became a force and turned the game completely on its head.

Sylvain Distin headed City back into the contest as he caught Spurs cold when Michael Tarnat clipped a free kick over the wall straight after the break.

Then, as Spurs were on the rack, Paul Bosvelt's strike from the edge of the box deflected past Kasey Keller off Anthony Gardner and eleven minutes from time Shaun Wright-Phillips chipped over the keeper.

Disbelieving Spurs fans were horrified, but there was one final twist to come. An injury-time cross from Michael Tarnat found the head of Jonathan Macken and the City substitute – on for the lacklustre Anelka – placed his effort perfectly into the far corner for a sensational winner.

It was typical City, and although David James and new centre-half Daniel van Buyten can come in, the bitter truth is that if they continue to defend as they did last night, they will need similar miracles for the rest of the season to get them out of trouble.

Spurs had begun their Carling Cup win over City in December with a goal inside two minutes, and when they did so again Keegan must have feared the worst.

New keeper Arni Arason, making his debut after his loan move from Rosenborg with James Cup-tied, had not touched the ball before he was picking it out of the City net as King followed Darren Anderton's December example.

The goal was a beauty too, with King linking up with Stephane Dalmat and latching on to the ball after Simon Davies prodded square, before turning inside Richard Dunne and thrashing home left-footed from eighteen yards.

After just one win in three months, it was exactly the start City did not need, and when Kasey Keller escaped when he seemed to claw down Sun Jihai after carelessly spilling the ball, Keegan's face showed the tension.

But it was Helder Postiga's hamstring that twanged first, the struggling striker forced to make way after just eight minutes for Gus Poyet. With Defoe in waiting and Fredi Kanoute returning from Africa later this month, the Portuguese frontman may be out of the frame for a long time. Spurs had to reorganise, although Keane's zest saw him wriggling clear to test Arason from twenty yards.

City came close to a leveller on thirteen minutes as Robbie Fowler, back up front after a replacement role at Highbury on Sunday, took advantage of Gardner's weak clearance to thump a volley that beat Keller all ends up yet flashed inches wide.

Fowler, looking really sharp, was raiding again three minutes later, bursting through the Spurs right and firing beyond Keller but also wide of the post.

Yet it was Spurs who struck again, with Keane's predatory instincts outstanding as he claimed his fifth goal in the last six games on nineteen minutes.

Stephen Carr's ball from half-way found Keane and he controlled it beautifully, sprinted between Distin and Dunne, cushioned the ball on the outside of his right foot and then lofted over Arason with his left.

When Anelka pulled up claiming his groin had gone after twenty-seven minutes, he did not exactly seem devastated. Ziege put all his injury horrors behind him with a vintage left-footed free kick which flew home after Barton was booked for a studs-up foul on Michael Brown twenty-two yards out.

Barton did not let the matter drop, and when he continued yapping away at the referee after the whistle, he was dismissed.

Keegan clearly got his men going in the dressing-room as they came out revved up. Distin's goal gave them a glimpse of a chance and Fowler almost forced his way through for another.

When Arason produced a magnificent double-save to foil Ziege's free kick and Poyet's follow-up header, City were still alive, and Bosvelt's deflected strike on the hour, Wright-Phillips' cool finish and Macken's precise header completed one of the most remarkable games in the rich history of the FA Cup.

FA Cup Fourth Round Replay

Tottenham... (3) 3	Man City... (0) 4
King 2	Distin 48
Keane 19	Bosvelt 61
Ziege 43	Wright-Phillips 80
	Macken 90

Att: 30,400

Wayne's World Begins

RUUD'S REVENGE

DUTCHMAN IS SPOT ON THIS TIME AS WENGER LEFT FUMING AT REFEREE

Manchester United 2 Arsenal 0

Martin Lipton

He should have ended the unbeaten run when it was just eight games old, not bring it to a close when it had already stretched for seventeen months.

But a year after he left the Old Trafford crossbar rocking from the spot at one end, Ruud van Nistelrooy kept his penalty firmly on the ground at the other to breathe life into Manchester United's championship pursuit of Arsenal – and indeed their whole season.

Arsenal's fury at referee Mike Riley was understandable, as he bought Wayne Rooney's tumble in the mere vicinity of Sol Campbell's trailing leg.

It was a shocking decision by any standards, made all the worse by Riley's history as United's secret weapon, the eighth spot kick he has given Sir Alex Ferguson's side in as many visits to Old Trafford.

What made it worse was that Arsenal were incensed that both van Nistelrooy and Rio Ferdinand were still on the pitch at all, the Dutchman after raking his foot down Ashley Cole's knee, and the otherwise outstanding United stand-in skipper

for a blatant professional foul on Freddie Ljungberg.

Yet for all the storm of protest, van Nistelrooy kept his nerve and ignored any memories to drill home past Jens Lehmann and gain revenge in the only way a striker can.

That Rooney claimed a nineteenth birthday present of his first Premiership goal for United in added time, sweeping home from Alan Smith's cross, only added to Old Trafford glee as they celebrated with relish the end of Arsenal's forty-nine-game unbeaten run.

Even in the absence of Roy Keane, Phil Neville – making only his second start of the season – and Paul Scholes just about kept Edu and Patrick Vieira in check.

While the tackles by the Neville brothers that Arsene Wenger argued were deliberate attempts to crock Jose Antonio Reyes were not pretty, they summed up the resolve of a side that could not consider defeat, especially against these opponents, seeking that statistical landmark.

And time and again, just as Arsenal's more cohesive, cogent and convincing football looked set to bring its reward, Ferdinand was there with a tackle, a block or an interception.

Of course, Ferdinand should not have been on the pitch beyond the nineteenth minute, after Edu's weighted pass sent Ljungberg bursting through the middle. The Swede got the touch as Ferdinand came across and there was cold-blooded cynicism about the bodycheck which followed.

Riley, fifteen yards away, simply waved play-on. How, only he will know. The Leeds official then missed van Nistelrooy's ugly lunge on Cole.

With seventeen minutes left, Rooney fed to Cristiano Ronaldo and moved smartly to take the return, yet what followed was proof that the boy has learned an old lag's tricks.

Campbell's leg was briefly outstretched but the centre-half had yanked it back in before Rooney had begun to fall to ground and was visibly admonishing his England colleague for the dive even as Riley pointed to the spot.

Amid the maelstrom, van Nistelrooy remained calm to score.

His only other Premiership goal this season was also from the spot against North London opposition but it is fair to

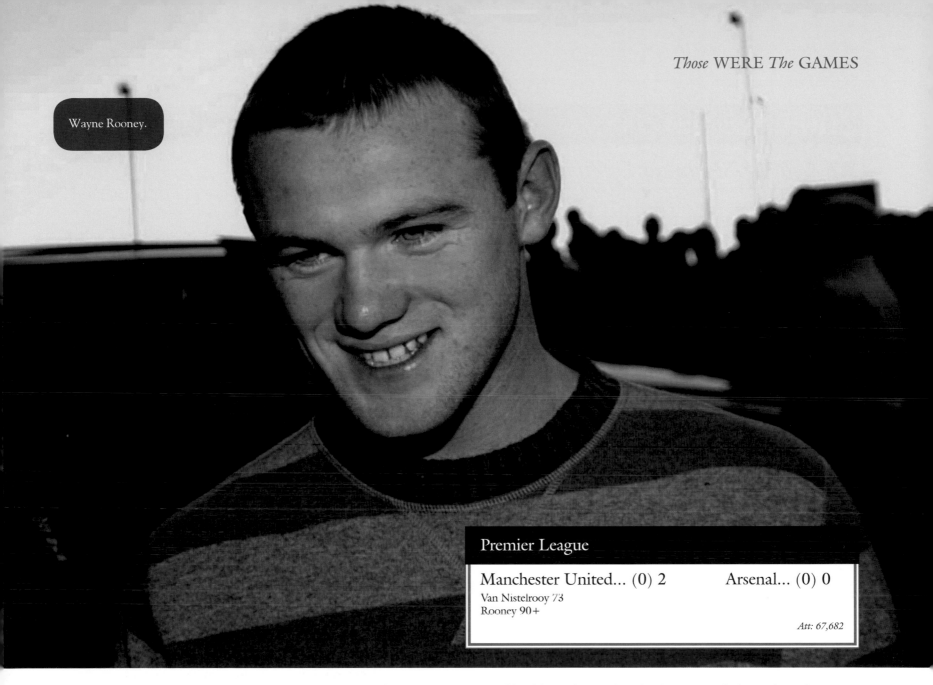

Wayne Rooney.

Premier League

Manchester United... (0) 2	Arsenal... (0) 0
Van Nistelrooy 73	
Rooney 90+	
	Att: 67,682

suggest the celebrations at White Hart Lane last month were restrained in contrast to the outpouring of joy here.

Cole escaped a cast-iron spot kick when he downed Ronaldo and Arsenal were now desperate, and open to the counter. Louis Saha found fellow replacement Smith on the right, and the low centre begged the assured finish from Rooney.

Campbell refused to shake Rooney's hand at the end, while Wenger marched on to let Riley know he felt "robbed".

Perhaps, though, the biggest winner of all was not van Nistelrooy or Fergie, but Jose Mourinho. Thanks to Riley,

United had kept themselves in the race. Chelsea, though, are racing to win, not for a place.

At least we still have three horses running.

POSTSCRIPT

The match ended in uproar when players and staff from both sides were involved in a furious tunnel bust up. Food and drink was hurled, and United manager Sir Alex Ferguson ended up with pizza thrown onto his face. The game has since been known as "Pizzagate"!

Yet Another Stunning Fightback

UNBELIEVABUL

LIVERPOOL THE KINGS OF EUROPE AFTER GREATEST FIGHTBACK IN CUP HISTORY

AC Milan 3 Liverpool 3

Martin Lipton

Liverpool sealed the greatest comeback in Champions League history last night to turn the Istanbul night red with Scousers' delight.

Rafa Benitez's men had stood on the brink of humiliation as they were three goals down before the break and being run ragged by the brilliance of Brazilian Kaka and the predatory instincts of Chelsea castoff Hernan Crespo.

But the legends of the past could only look on in wonder as the Reds turned a lost cause into a night of sheer bedlam in the space of six stunning minutes that defied belief and all footballing logic.

And then just as against Roma twenty-one years ago, the Reds triumphed from the spot again, as Jerzy Dudek proved the hero in a penalty shoot-out as Liverpool won it 3-2.

Benitez, horribly let down by Harry Kewell who repaid his decision to back the Aussie over Didi Hamann by limping away after twenty-three minutes, looked to have made a mistake that might haunt him for years.

A first-minute goal from Paolo Maldini seemed to have knocked the stuffing out of the Reds, while the absence of Hamann allowed the inspirational Kaka to rip huge holes in the Liverpool rearguard.

When Crespo, on loan from Chelsea and still having half his £90,000-per-week wages paid by the Blues, capitalised twice on Kaka's approach work, the Special One's castoff appeared to be gaining Stamford Bridge revenge for the semi-final defeat.

Yet out of nowhere, Liverpool found the courage and guts to change everything as Steven Gerrard's header sparked a comeback that would have been dismissed as fanciful in a *Boy's Own* comic.

Kewell's replacement, Vladimir Smicer, grabbed a second and as the Liverpool fans began to urge their men onwards, Gerrard's run into the box was ended by a foul from Rino Gattuso and Xabi Alonso converted the rebound after Dida saved his spot kick.

The Merseyside fans who filled three-quarters of the ground had believed in glorious victory. But those dreams were looking shattered as Milan struck a devastating blow inside 53 seconds. Djimi Traore had no need to jump in on Kaka as the Brazilian was wandering rather aimlessly on the right-flank. When he did so, the consequences were brutal.

Andrea Pirlo sized up his options before delivering to the penalty spot and, despite a host of red shirts, it was the right boot of Maldini that connected, his downward volley bouncing past the unprepared Dudek.

Gerrard and Alonso were struggling to get any sort of grip on proceedings, with the cowardly Kewell letting down Liverpool and Benitez as he seemed to be looking for a way out even before the groin knock that saw him make way for Smicer. The boos and jeers from the Liverpool fans told their own story.

Milan were looking to get in behind Liverpool at every opportunity, sharper to the ball and far more controlled and

dangerous, and when the sublime Kaka slipped Shevchenko through on goal on twenty-eight minutes, the Ukrainian did not expect the flag to be raised as he reeled away in triumph after slotting home.

Liverpool, by contrast, were hitting with hope rather than expectation, although neat work between Riise and Baros gave Garcia a rare sight of goal, his volley slicing wide.

But it was what happened in the space of fifteen seconds in the thirty-eighth minute that seemed to have killed off Liverpool. Alonso sent Garcia scurrying away in to the box, his shift inside sending Alessandro Nesta on to his back as the ball clearly struck the defender's arm inside the box.

Yet neither referee Manuel Mejuto Gonzalez nor his assistant spotted the blatant handball and Milan struck with devastating efficiency as Kaka's ball to Shevchenko found that gap behind Traore.

Jamie Carragher's momentary loss of balance made the task easy for the Argentine. And two minutes before the break, Kaka unhinged the Reds with a sublime turn away from Gerrard, matched by a peerless pass that sent Crespo romping away.

The finish was deadly and instant, Dudek helpless as the ball was scooped over him to nestle in the bottom corner. Yet the introduction of Hamann sparked the most astonishing turnaround in the fifty-year history of the Cup.

When Gerrard rose unattended to meet Riise's cross with a looping header that billowed into the net, it looked like a consolation act.

But it galvanised Liverpool and breathed life into their fans. Within two minutes, Smicer's drilled effort from twenty yards sneaked past Dida to finish in the bottom corner.

Then Garcia's touch sent Gerrard in on goal, with Rino Gattuso clearly bundling him over.

This time the referee pointed to the spot and, although Dida saved Alonso's initial spot kick, the midfielder rammed the rebound into the roof of the net. But there was more spot-kick drama to come as Liverpool triumphed.

UEFA Champions League Final	
AC Milan... (3) 3	**Liverpool... (0) 3**
Maldini 1	Gerrard 54
Crespo 39, 44	Smicer 56
	Alonso 59
Aet. 3-3 after 90 mins. Liverpool win 3-2 on pens.	
	Att: 65,000

One of the *Daily Mirror*'s greatest football writers, Frank McGhee in 1972.